The Heart of Pickleball

Personal stories that helped create the pickleball craze

By Fran Scharf and Eve Hanna, MD

The Heart of Pickleball

Cover by Divya Mohan
Printed by BookBaby

ISBN: 979-8-35096-849-1

We dedicate this book in memory of Jan Abbott, founding member of the Brunswick Forest Pickleball Club and founder and managing director of the House of Pickleball in Leland, NC. He inspired many to discover joy in life through hobbies and sports, especially pickleball. Truly a life well lived, and the world is a little less bright without him. He will be greatly missed.

Contents

Acknowledgements

We would like to thank all of the wonderful pickleballers who shared their personal stories for our book. The input from your pickleball experiences are what brought out the heart of pickleball.

We are also grateful for those of you who gave of your time for in-depth interviews. Your stories added such great detail to the development of the sport.

We would like to give a huge thank you to Gillian Smit and Divya Mohan for their vision and assistance with our editing, layout, and book cover design. They were crucial in making this book a reality.

We want to give a big shout out to our friends who spent time reading our book and making helpful suggestions and to our husbands who supported us throughout this year long process.

Introduction

Greetings from your pickleball-obsessed authors, Eve and Fran. We met on the pickleball court in Wilmington, North Carolina, and bonded over both being left-handed. While playing together one day, Fran hit the ball down the middle and said, "Down the middle, solves the riddle." Eve replied with, "Hit it where they aren't." Fran said, "We should put those words of wisdom in a book about pickleball."

So that's what we've included, along with other interesting tidbits about the pickleball craze. We started with a few thoughts of our own, but then we got the bright idea to ask players for their input. We put together a survey about the different aspects of the sport, gave it to our friends and strangers, put out questions on social media sites, and started collecting stories.

What we discovered was that pickleball was more than just a game. It was a cascade of fun and positivity that resulted in life changes for some and a sense of well-being for all. We created this book to share that heart of pickleball with you. Enjoy!

The Heart of Pickleball: A Poem
By Chat GPT

In the sun-drenched courts of summer's eve,
Where laughter echoes and paddles weave,
A game is played with skill and grace,
Where pickleballers find their place.
A fusion of tennis, badminton too,
This sport is born of something new,
With paddles swift and balls that fly,
The game is fast, the action high.
The court is small, the net is low,
But energy and passion flow,
As players move with nimble feet,
And send the ball with perfect beat.

The volleys fly, the points accrue,
As players try to bring to view,
Their best in every shot they take
And never let their focus break.
And so the game goes on and on,
With players striving until dawn,
To be the one who claims the prize,
And in the end, to realize.
That in this game of skill and sight,
Where players fight with all their might,
The truest victory is this:
To play with heart and never miss!

Chapter 1

The Pickleball Craze

Why is pickleball the fastest growing pastime since baseball? One reason is that it takes us back to a time when we could pick up a ball and stick and go play a game for hours.

Remember when you could just go to "the place" and there was a game to be played? Baseball on the sandlot, roller hockey on your street, or pick-up basketball at the park. You would walk to the playing field and just start playing. With pickleball, we have a pick-up activity again, and it feels so good.

But we knew that wasn't all there was to the attraction. So, we took to the streets and asked, "Why do you think there is such a pickleball craze now?" The responses were similar and touched on several common themes.

Pickleball Is A Social Sport

There is an instant group connection. The smaller court keeps you in close proximity with others and contributes to the social aspect of the game. Open play gives you an opportunity to meet new people.

Pickleball Is Easy To Learn

The smaller paddle and smaller court make it easier to learn and play than tennis. There are many people who are not necessarily athletic that play and enjoy recreational pickleball. Anyone can learn it, even if they haven't had any ball sports experience. It is more social than competitive, so men and women can play together. It's an easy sport to learn if you have basic hand–eye coordination. People who don't consider themselves athletes can feel accomplished in a sport while enjoying all the benefits of regular exercise.

Pickleball Is Good Exercise

Walking or running for an hour a day may get boring. Lifting weights may get boring. Playing pickleball for an hour a day is fun, and who plays pickleball for just an hour? Pickleball burns a lot more calories, and puts less strain on the body. It brings out the competitive spirit in a positive way. It is simply a better way for people to exercise and be healthy.

Pickleball Is Inclusive For All

A person of any age can play the game, from kids to older adults. Anyone who is moderately healthy can play, learn to improve, and have fun. Any body type can play, and it also works for those who are physically limited. You don't have to look like Barbie. Individuals of any skill level can find players with similar skills and enjoy the game at that level.

Pickleball Brings Joy

There are lots of laughs and smiles on the court. It makes you feel happy! It is addictive. It reminds us of the fun we had as kids at recess.

"The craze has been happening quietly for many years and is now rapidly accelerating in popularity. In 2014, I spoke with a housing developer friend in Florida who said he would never build another community without pickleball courts."

—Kim

Pickleball Or Tennis, Anyone? [1]

Jason Gay wrote a piece in the *Wall Street Journal* about the pickleball craze. He said the phenomenon is undeniable. The oft-repeated phrase is "the fastest growing sport in America," although to be fair, there isn't much competition. Everywhere you look, there are courts full of people playing pickleball while surrounding athletic fields sit barren.

As the momentum picks up, celebrities are getting involved. Leonardo DiCaprio plays, George Clooney plays, Emma Watson plays, Jamie Foxx sells paddles, and Billie Eilish's brother, Finneas, installed a court at his new home. Many stars have signed on as shareholders of pro teams, including Tom Brady, LeBron James, Patrick Mahomes, Eva Longoria, and Heidi Klum.

Some will argue that pickleball has no aesthetic merits. There's no elegance like that found in center court or any movement in pickleball as pretty as a Roger Federer backhand. But pickleball thrives because it's casual, devoid of stuffiness or even athletic prerequisites. It isn't trying to be tennis. It's trying to be fun and succeeding!

The future of pickleball is being played up the street from me and you. It's open to a hard-core athlete who wants to hit seven times a week and a barefoot vacationer who just picked up a paddle for the first time, maybe after a few margaritas. Pickleball is showing genuine, grassroots, exponential growth. The name may sound funny, but the craze is authentic!

Tina's Story

Alan and I teamed up when the town of Norwalk, Connecticut, decided to build four pickleball courts in early 2022. We had no idea what an incredible community would develop, but we both had a similar vision for the future of the park. While Woodward Park is owned by Norwalk, the town was not ready to run or organize the details of pickleball play.

Alan and I knew how to use the TeamReach app to connect to interested people. We understood how to organize level play. We both were familiar with open play, which no one had heard of in the Northeast and we had a good understanding of how to run it. We never would have imagined so many people being on our TeamReach.

It is exciting that we have over 1800 group members now. We have dozens of people come and play every day. They even bring their own nets because four courts are not enough most days. We have a wide range of age groups from ten to eighty plus years old. We have had college nights, ladies nights, and have hosted tournaments. There are so many great things happening at Woodward Park.

We do have some people who are on our TeamReach, not to play but to see how it's done. Many town officials and other pickleballers are trying figure out how to use TeamReach to organize play in their local areas. They want to know what our trick is to having so many people come to open play at each level. They want to have the same kind of amazing energy we have. Some days, when Alan and I reflect on all of the joy we see every day, we think, OMG, this is such a special place for so many people!

Carol's Story

Playing pickleball on a regular basis doesn't cost much. You can buy a paddle and balls at any sporting goods store, general discount store, or online. You can play in most any city for free outdoors and at an affordable cost indoors. It is a win-win sport—spend a little and play a lot.

"The pandemic sped up the pickleball craze that had already begun. People seeking exercise and socialization were able to play pickleball as it was 'COVID-friendly.'"

—Jesse

Peggy's Story

When I moved to a new area, I developed an almost instant group of pickleball friends who are positive, healthy, and imaginative. Whenever I have traveled to other places, I've joined in with other welcoming pickleball players on their courts. The sport attracts enthusiastic people. Maybe it's church 2023?

As more and more people experience the joy and accessibility of pickleball, the word is spreading exponentially. I know I reach out to most people I come in contact with about playing pickleball. There are minimal costs and minimal previous athletic abilities needed to play, with great rewards. Individuals of any age can learn it, even if they haven't had any previous ball sports experience. People of any skill level can find like-level players to play the game.

Credit: Larry Scharf

Pickleball inspires people to think outside of the box and do some crazy things!

Chapter 2

Pickleball Crazy

The Pickleball Pilot

When Dean Matt, aka "The Pickleball Pilot," and his wife moved to Florida from the Midwest for recreation, their plans took a surprise turn. "We moved to a golf course community, because we thought we would be playing golf," Dean said, "but instead, we've been playing pickleball."

Dean combined his love of flying and his pickleball addiction to set a world record. He played pickleball games in forty-four states in thirty days! Most days, he played in two different states; some days, it was three different states.

A pilot since high school, he flew his Turbo Cessna 206H six-passenger aircraft 8,122 nautical miles and logged eighty-two hours of flight time for this challenge. Dean was joined by fellow pilots, members from the pickleball community, his wife, and others at various stops along the way.

Dean's trip began on May 1, 2023, from Southwest Florida to his first stop in Mobile, Alabama. He then marched southwestward across the United States, looped up toward Washington state, continued eastward through the Plains and Midwest, scooted southward along the East Coast, and ended in a final match in Sarasota, Florida, where he lives. The route included fifteen state capitals, a few Chicken N Pickle restaurants, lots of tennis centers, and a motor home resort in South Carolina.

"The event was mainly to showcase all the different places pickleball is played," Dean said. Throughout his journey, he played with a variety of people in public parks, at private clubs and homes, and even on an airport tarmac. He's played against professional pickleball players, local players, and celebrities.

At his stop in Virginia Beach, Dean played against former Virginia governor and the United States senator George Allen. He played with a ninety-seven-year-old woman in Kalamazoo, Michigan. In Wilmington, North Carolina, he played with Wayne Bigg from the Cape Fear Pickleball Club. The duo faced off against City Council member Clifford Barnett and Jimmy Santangelo, a pickleball player who met up with Dean at his Rhode Island stop and played the last eight states with him.

Originally, Dean and his friend, Shannon Yeager, a professional private pilot and pickleball player, wanted to set a Guinness World Record by playing one game of pickleball in each of the forty-eight contiguous United States over a forty-eight-day period. When Shannon had to bow out of the adventure due to a business commitment, Dean felt it would have been disingenuous to continue to attempt a Guinness World Record.

Dean's favorite parts of the trip are the people he has met and the places he has seen along the way. What a great way to get the word out about pickleball all around America!

"On Thursday, May 25, 2023, Dean flew to Wilmington, North Carolina from Virginia Beach for a game of pickleball. All of us spectators were thrilled that he chose our city and enjoyed the game and the hoopla of the event. The historical happening was hosted by the Cape Fear Pickleball Club and was well covered by our local news media."

—Carol, Social Events Chairman,
Cape Fear Pickleball Club

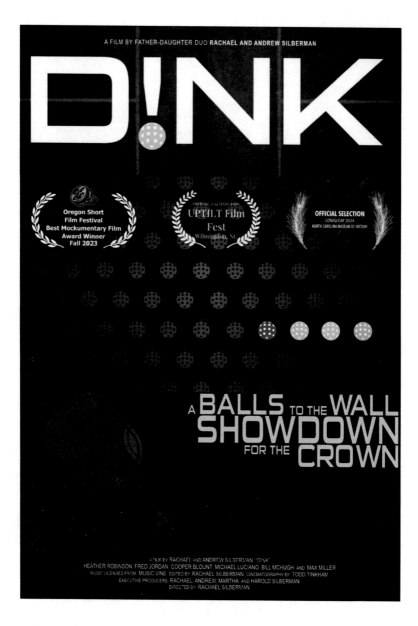

You can keep up with all of the showings and awards for Dink at
www.dinktheshortfilm.com

Pickleball Gets Its Name in Lights

Rachael Silberman and her dad showcased their love of pickleball by writing and producing a short film about the sport called *Dink*, a pickleball comedy. It is about the "Grab the Gherkin" Pickleball Tournament that comes to Wilmington, North Carolina. In the film, four regional champions enter to compete for the Grand Gherkin Trophy and become legends in pickleball history.

Rachael Silberman is an award-winning filmmaker with four short films to her credit. She and her pickleball-addicted dad, Andrew or, "Sir Lobs a Lot," wrote, cast, directed, and produced *Dink*. Their short film won the Best Mockumentary Film Award at the fall 2023 Oregon Short Film Festival.

Pickleball had become part of the Silbermans' lives several years earlier when Rachael's parents moved to Compass Point in Wilmington, North Carolina. Andrew loved basketball, but back issues took him out of the game.

"I felt like over the past ten years, my dad just wanted something to get back into and he hadn't found it yet," Rachael said. "When he moved to Compass Point, he found pickleball and it totally changed him. He gets so much joy from playing, he's lost so much weight, he's never looked better, and he's so excited. Pickleball has given him his life back."

Rachael has caught the pickleball bug as well, though on a far more social and casual basis. She plays when she visits her parents or has free time. But she will admit that it's in her blood and she has a little addiction. While she doesn't watch all the latest YouTube videos that her father does, she is all about the "Let's go, I want to play now, and I want to teach you" mentality.

One day, she saw the young sheriff who lives across the hall from her with a paddle in his hand. When she asked where he was headed, he said he was going to play pickleball. As it turned out, he had never played before. She offered to join him and teach him the rules.

"There are rules?" he said. "I was just going to smack the ball around for a bit." She set him straight and off they went to play. According to Rachael, "Everyone who plays seems to get a new lease on life. It is truly a positive experience."

While Rachael was laid up from a broken leg (not a pickleball injury), her dad said, "Wouldn't it be great fun to do a spoof about pickleball? Then we would have a project we could do together like in the past." She thought it could be fun but reminded him that making an independent film is a big undertaking and takes a lot of prep work and a lot of money.

First they talked about the spoof concept and how they loved the movie *Best in Show* and slapstick comedies like *Dodgeball*. Rachael said she probably wrote most of the script and her dad came in with the last twenty-five percent to help "zhuzh" it up.

They decided to film it at the House of Pickleball in Leland, North Carolina, using local cast and crew as well as family and friends to complete the project. They held casting calls, hired the crew, and recruited extras from local pickleball clubs, friends, and family members. A local councilman has a role in the film, and Benny's Pizza, a local pizza joint, got to be in the movie as well.

"There was this wise-guy-type from Compass Point," Rachael recalls. "He was a typical guy from New York or New Jersey. He was just wonderful, and we used his persona as one of the main characters. Basically, I told him, "We'll write lines for you, but you need to be who you are."

When they held casting calls, only he and one other actor knew how to play pickleball. The other two main characters had never played the game.

As the days of filming moved on, everyone learned what pickleball was and how to play the game, and everyone became addicted. "Initially the crew knew nothing about pickleball, and then they got really into it," Rachael said. "During the off times when they weren't shooting, the crew could be found playing."

As Rachael told her story, her emotion and excitement were palpable. It was obvious that the community she had created while making this film had moved her and the others involved, fostering friendships and camaraderie.

"What a labor of love this was to work with my dad," she said. "He was so excited about the project and his fire was so contagious. Honestly, it was a joy."

We've Played (Almost) Everywhere

Mari Jo's story

We've all heard that you can't have your cake and eat it too! That might be true most of the time, but there can be exceptions. Recently, we found an amazing way to put two of our greatest passions, travel and pickleball together. We weren't going to postpone one dream while undertaking the other or choose one over the other.

It all started in 2017 when I asked my husband, Rich, what he would like for Christmas, and he said, "Something we can do together." Although we had never tried the game, I chose to give him a pickleball paddle for Christmas, and we haven't stopped playing since.

We are fortunate to have lots of time together on the courts as Rich is retired from a career in computer programming and I am a retired public health nurse. We met in a church choir where we both played guitar and have been married for over thirty years.

While fulfilling our travel dreams and enjoying the irresistible game of pickleball, we have found our favorite places to play, met wonderful people, and formed friendships that have endured both on and off the courts.

When wanderlust takes over and we go off on a road trip, we now seek out pickleball venues where we can get in a game or two during our trips around the country.

It got to the point where we never leave home without our paddles. In the spring of 2023, on a trip down to Florida to visit family, we got the notion that we could try to play pickleball in all fifty states of the U.S.A. By the time we hit North Carolina, we realized that we already had eight states under our belt. Only forty-two to go!

When we got home from that trip, we were up to eleven states and more motivated than ever. At the pickleball courts in North Carolina, we casually mentioned to another player that we aspired to play in all fifty states. The news spread, and we were interviewed for a news article in North Carolina. It ran in the local paper and hit the *Associated Press*.

Much to our surprise, the article spread far and wide and resulted in an invitation for us to go out to Nebraska to play at a phenomenal sports facility in the city of Papillion. It took no time at all for us to accept the invitation, pack our bags, and head west.

During that trip in June 2023, we bagged thirteen more states, bringing us to the halfway mark. Later we were able to cross Maine off our list, for a total of twenty-six states. Our next major venture is to drive out to the Grand Canyon, which we have never visited, and play the game in seventeen more states.

Lots of pickleball enthusiasts ask us how many matches we play when we travel and how we go about finding the courts in each state. Our personal convention is that we play at least one doubles game in a state to "count" that state as completed. Apart from Nebraska, where we were invited to play, we go to the pickleball courts in each state pretty much "cold," without any games pre-arranged.

We do research on our own ahead of time, using the internet to search for parks, community centers, YMCAs, and clubs that offer pickleball. Then we just show up during open play and mingle with the local pickleball community. The players are always welcoming and make us feel as comfortable as if we were on our "home court." This is one of the beautiful aspects of pickleball.

While this journey has given us a way to realize both our travel dreams and our pickleball aspirations, there is another reason why we are committed to accomplishing our fifty state pickleball challenge. We are on this quest to celebrate the life-changing game of pickleball and how it is bringing people together across our nation.

Pickleball is a game for people of all ages and physical abilities. It offers health, social, and recreational benefits to those who participate in the game at all levels. In our travels, we have been thrilled to find the ever-growing interest and participation in this sport, as well as the proliferation of great places to play. We are grateful to live in this magnificent country and to have the opportunity to play pickleball from sea to shining sea.

"Now, we are seeing the United States of America, one pickleball court at a time."

—Mari Jo

Suncoast Pickleball Association

Chapter 3

The First Time

Everyone remembers their first time! First steps, first time riding a bike, first love, first team sport, first kiss, and first time on the pickleball court are memorable events. It is amazing how many people become smitten right from the start.

Fran's Story

I had just moved to a new community in North Carolina. I had never heard of pickleball, but my walking partner had picked it up and spoke about it avidly. Every time I heard her speak about it, I disliked the sport even more (which I had never seen or played). Then the pandemic hit and all sources of socializing were shut down except for golf, tennis, and pickleball.

My obvious path of least resistance was pickleball. So, I went to my first pickleball open play. No one was more surprised than I was, but right then and there, I was hooked. I had never been an athlete, and I couldn't believe the feelings I was having—endorphins, camaraderie, competitiveness—all of the above? Who knew I wanted those things?

I started playing every day. I had to get better. I had to know more about this game. I became a pickleball addict. A couple of years have gone by, and I am still addicted.

One of the benefits for me, after struggling with my weight all of my life, was that I had become forty pounds lighter. My bone density tests showed a ten percent increase and my heart age decreased by four years, which for a sixty-year-old woman, I guess isn't that common. But best of all, I no longer have to do that three-mile walk/run, hoping it will effect a change.

Thank you, pickleball—you gave me my physical health, without me having to think about it.

Walt's Story

My wife, Janie, and I were looking to retire from the northern Virginia area, and we toured many communities that had pickleball. We had never played pickleball before, but I had played racquetball, and it looked like the game was fun. To get a feel for the community we were visiting, I would stop by the pickleball courts and ask the players about their community, its highlights and lowlights.

Everyone was very open and friendly! I think we got a good appreciation of the folks in the community from the pickleball players, and this factored into our ultimate "where should we move to" decision. Within a month of moving, I attended a new player pickleball class. After a couple of introductory sessions, I was hooked!

Maureen's Story

I heard about the game of pickleball and it sounded cool. I searched for places near me, found a place and started playing, and I enjoyed it. I am in a senior's group in my small town of 5000 people and the group was looking for activities for seniors.

I recommended pickleball and got us a place to play indoors. Another person who had been playing had a net and paddles, and so we started playing outdoors as well. Now the town has given us six outdoor courts and we have 100 people on our list of players.

Peg's Story

Sometimes the first time on the pickleball court is challenging because there is no court!

My husband, Les and I have played pickleball for about seven and a half years. We were introduced to the game in a brief conversation during a visit with friends in Florida. The wife was not home when we arrived, and we were told she was off playing pickleball. Well of course the name piqued our curiosity, and we asked her about it when she returned.

The game seemed intriguing, and when we arrived back in North Carolina, we started to look into it. We invested in a game set that included a portable net, end bases that you filled with sand, and plywood paddles. My husband and one of our neighbors went out and did nothing more than hit the ball back and forth for several weeks. Meanwhile, we started to research the general rules.

We were not aware of any pickleball courts anywhere in our area, although we had tennis courts at our clubhouse. After a few weeks, we decided that we needed to lay out the court dimensions on one of our tennis courts. We measured out the court perimeter using a sharpie to mark the corners of the outside lines and then the kitchen and center lines.

At the time, our best option was to snap chalk lines on the tennis court. Needless to say, this did not go over well with some of the tennis players! Then we purchased bright yellow rubber corners and straight pieces specifically for pickleball. Now, we were ready to play.

We had graduated to fiberglass paddles and were playing singles for several months when our friend found out there were indoor courts not too far from our neighborhood. A local church allowed to play several afternoons a week, with one day designated for beginners and other days for more advanced players. The three of us enthusiastically headed to the beginners' play and the new world of doubles play. Another first-time event!

After our second session, the pickleball play organizer told us we were ready to move up to the next level. While we could hit the ball well and knew the basic rules, we were novices at doubles play and lacking in the subtleties of team play. After several weeks of playing multiple times per week, we finally got the hang of it. This began an ongoing obsession for playing multiple times a week at multiple venues.

We have been successful in getting the tennis court in our neighborhood lined for pickleball and we have progressed to more sophisticated paddles and equipment. We spend our days looking for materials to make outdoor play easier and more comfortable, including ball and paddle holders. We now have awnings and fans (some that spray water) for the summer months and cold weather gear for the winter months.

We started with a small number of players and now have groups with over sixty people on the roster. Quite a change from three intrepid players braving cold and heat on a chalk-lined court.

Carol's Story

Initially it was curiosity. 'What is pickleball?' I wanted to know. I started going off and on once a week in 2013 but I was inconsistent due to a hectic life with children and aging parents. In 2021, we moved to North Carolina and I needed a way to meet people. Pickleball was the way to do that and now I'm curious, "What is life without pickleball?" Boring is the answer!

Steve's Story

Just over two years ago I went to the House of Pickleball because I heard about this game that was a combination of tennis, racquetball, and Ping-Pong. I'd played all three of those sports in the past so I thought I would give it a try. As a life-long competitive Ping-Pong player who had to give it up at the age of 50 due to the need for progressive lenses for my vision, I thought pickleball could be a great replacement. I played once and I was hooked!

Jesse's Story

My poker group consisted of twelve to fifteen 30- to 40-year-old men. My neighbor hosted some of these gatherings and had a connection to a private retirement community. The community had some of the only courts around at the time. I was playing tennis then and quickly found pickleball to be more social and fun.

JoAnn's Story

I traveled to Florida to a community that had pickleball courts. Our friends invited us to play, and we were hooked! We came back to North Carolina and immediately asked the leadership of our community's fitness center to install some pickleball courts. I became so enthralled with the sport that my husband and I became part owners of a pickleball facility.

Kim's Story

I started playing pickleball in Bonita Springs, Florida, ten years ago when it was offered at our club. I was a tennis player for over 40 years but decided to give pickleball a try. I enjoyed it immediately! I went home for the summer to Connecticut and looked for places to play. No one had even heard of pickleball. It took until the COVID-19 pandemic for the sport to gain ground in Connecticut when people were looking for safe activities outdoors.

Eve's Story

When we moved to North Carolina, my husband and I became preview members at the club in our area and were interested in what they had to offer. They sponsored an "intro to pickleball" lesson on a converted tennis court. It was fun from the get-go and easy to pick up the basics right away, except for the scoring. I was never sure where I was supposed to be for 0-0 Start.

After our lesson, the instructor told us about a beginner's group at the Lutheran church nearby. I started playing there regularly, learned the rules, and finally understood the scoring system. It was great because I got to play with other folks who were just starting out as well.

I had never played a team sport before. My foray into athletics consisted of being on the swim team and taking dance classes. It was exciting to think I was part of a sport that included partner strategy and the option to be on a team and compete in tournaments.

We all have different stories about our first time, but they end exactly the same: "We're hooked!"

The Invention Of Pickleball

The history of pickleball is as unique and fun as the sport. In 1965 on Bainbridge Island near Seattle, Washington, Frank Pritchard was 13 and bored. He challenged his father, Representative Joel Pritchard, to make up a game, and Joel accepted the dare. To paraphrase Plato, boredom is the mother of invention. Who knew this creative mishmash of Ping-Pong, badminton, and tennis would become an international sensation!

Joel and his friend, Bill Bell, started gathering up equipment: a badminton net, some table tennis paddles, and a whiffle ball. They set up the game on the Pritchard's' backyard badminton court and adjusted the height of the pickleball net to thirty-six inches, roughly the distance from the ground to Joel Pritchard's waist. The "kitchen" was developed to give some breathing room from Dick Brown, his six-foot-four-inch friend who would run up to the net and spike the ball.

They found that the whiffle ball bounced well on the asphalt but the paddles kept breaking. They enlisted the help of their friend, Barney McCallum, who was able to make some more reliable paddles. Barney McCallum's skills would lead to the creation of the Pickle-ball, Inc. company in 1977, which sold a starter set of four wooden paddles, a net, and balls for $29.50. The three men created the rules and refined the game, always keeping in mind its original purpose as a game that the whole family could play.

They needed a name for their new family sport. Joel's wife, Joan Pritchard, came up with "pickleball," inspired by the leftover rowers who would race for fun in pickle boats after the main varsity team competition. The name stuck, and pickleball was born!

Fast forward three years to when the Pritchards invited Dick and Joan Brown and their children to the Bainbridge home. That summer, Paul Brown and Jeannie Pritchard were both ten years old. On one of their walks, they came across a litter of puppies and brought two of them home. The Browns named their puppy Lulu, and the Pritchards named their puppy Pickles.

Around 1970, Joel Pritchard was interviewed by a reporter from a national publication. He told the true story of how pickleball got its name, but also proposed that the game was named after Pickles the dog as a fun alternate story. The reporter went with the dog story version, and that's why many people think pickleball was named after the Pritchard's' dog.

Years later, Joel would tell the true story, but by then, the myth had become reality. Frank Pritchard feels strongly about giving his mother credit for naming the game, so pass along the real story of the naming of pickleball.

In 1976, the first pickleball tournament was held at the South Center Athletic Club in Tukwila, Washington. The men's doubles winners were Scott Stover and Rob Cahill. Scott Stover's wife was a second cousin of Barney McCallum, one of the founders of pickleball. Both Scott and Rob played many pickleball games on the original pickleball court on Bainbridge Island.

Pickleball was introduced into the schools in Washington, Oregon, and Idaho and played indoors in PE class as the sport began its march across the country. Joel Pritchard would set up pickleball games at his political rallies using members of the audience! By 1990, pickleball was being played in all fifty states.

National Pickleball Day was created in 2021 by Deirdre Morris, a pickleball instructor. She chose August 8 as the day to share her love for the sport and encourage others to learn and play. Pickleball continues to increase in popularity thanks to the Ambassador Program and opportunities to play within community centers, PE classes, YMCA facilities, and retirement communities.

Scott Stover (left) and Rob Cahill (right)
Men's doubles champions 1976

To find a place to play, check out the website
places2play.org

Rob Cahill, pointing out his image on the original box set

Chapter 4

Movers and Shakers

We found a group of people so inspired by their love of pickleball they were compelled to reach out and help others through the game. These people are using the sport as a vehicle to promote wellness, develop a sense of community, and effect change. We hope you find their stories as moving as we did.

House Of Pickleball

The Tres Amigos: Jan, Richard, and Marty

What do you get when you cross a car salesman with a software guru and a serial entrepreneur? You get the House of Pickleball (HOP) in Leland, North Carolina, the nonalcoholic Cheers. The HOP was the first indoor pickleball facility in the state when it opened in 2018.

The story begins several years earlier. Jan and Marty met by chance when they moved into the same neighborhood in a planned community called Brunswick Forest. Richard joined the group a couple of years later when he moved into the same community.

In 2012, Jan and his wife went to a Super Bowl party in Florida where there were pickleball courts. He played a little over the weekend and was hooked. He returned home and convinced the developer to set up lines on a tennis court, which gave them two pickleball courts. These are thought to be the first outdoor courts in the state and remain in use today.

It is not clear how Marty ended up on the courts for his first time, but both Jan and he remember that he took out the perimeter fence going for a ball. He, too, was hooked immediately. That same year, Marty became a USA Pickleball Ambassador, and his mission was to teach pickleball to as many people as he could, free of charge. Marty, along with other picklers that he was able to recruit, went to every community in Brunswick County.

"We would go out and chalk off the courts," Marty remembers. "We would bring nets, paddles, and balls with us." There would often be twenty-five to thirty people at a session. Marty and his crew were playing seven to eight times a week and training people several times a week. They were all in.

Even with the growing interest Marty and his group were creating and the hundreds of people they were introducing to the game, they still had a few issues holding them back from this new "calling." The first barrier concerned pickleball paddles. They were impossible to find anywhere but online, and in 2013 people were hesitant to buy paddles that way.

Jan made a call and quickly was able to secure a deal with Prolite paddles that allowed them to become a distributor of paddles. Marty would pack forty to fifty paddles into his van when he went to visit a community. He would let everyone try different paddles and buy their favorite one at the end.

Another challenge was that new pickleball players wanted more instruction than just the introductory lessons. Jan, who was a tennis instructor in another lifetime, became a pickle-ball instructor and offered lessons to any new players eager to improve their skills.

There was still no dedicated place to play, but these guys were not deterred. Marty went to the developers of Bruns-wick Forest with a presentation to convince them to build six pickleball courts. He told them to go down to Florida and visit The Villages, where pickleball rules!

The developers actually went, and when they returned, they built those six courts. They were so convinced of the growth of the sport that they changed their marketing strate-gy and started highlighting pickleball, bringing Marty along for their company's sales pitch for future developments.

Richard entered the scene in 2015. He sold his business and moved to Brunswick Forest to be closer to his grand-children. He had been an avid tennis player, and shortly after moving in, he took a break from unpacking and went down to the tennis courts to hit a few balls. When he was head-ing home, he noticed a couple of men playing "the stupidest game I ever saw." He did stop and ask about it, though, and the guys who were playing encouraged him to try it out. He was hooked that day and hasn't been on a tennis court since.

It was soon after this that Jan and Richard looked at each other and knew they had to capitalize on all their hard work. They were hooking thirty-five to forty people a week, but still had no place to play the game. They had a new mission: cre-ate a dedicated place to play!

"I spent three to four months riding every road in the county," Richard said, "but there was not a single suitable building for this type of endeavor." He and Jan put a plan to-gether to buy the land and build the HOP. It would have six indoor courts and allow players to reserve a court or show up for open play, sign up for a lesson or clinic, and enjoy playing pickleball for a few bucks while having a ball.

Richard called a meeting of all the ambassadors in the county to share their vision. When he showed them their proposal to build an indoor pickleball facility, they said, "You are crazy as hell! There is no way you're going to raise the money to do that, count us out."

But Richard was not to be deterred. He went back to each of the local communities and gave presentations to make people aware of their idea. He didn't ask them for money, just their time and attention. The first thing he showed them was the woods and the swamp around it, but once they saw the proposed concept of the facility, there was buy-in and tremendous participation.

It took them about three years to raise the money. Finally, in July 2018, their dreams became a reality and a pickleball community was created. The place was hopping immediately!

Just five years later, the need was so great that they opened up six more courts. When you walk into the HOP, you feel the energy and excitement immediately. There are always people coming and going, laughing and hanging out, from bright-eyed newbies ready to learn to players preparing for their next tournament. The place is full of love, laughter, and activity. Jan and Richard are instructors while Marty sells paddles and looks for the next champion. It keeps them all young, connected, and active.

As they shared their story, they played off of each other, bouncing between events and "remember when?" as tears flowed from both memories and laughter. They spoke about how pickleball was the foundation of the love they share, the friendships they have built, and the good and bad times that changed each of them for the better. Their efforts have left an indelible mark on thousands of lives by introducing pickleball to Brunswick Forest and beyond.

Pickleball Paddles Parkinson's

Scott Rider

I am sixty-four years old, I was forty-seven when I was diagnosed with Parkinson's disease. Sports or anything that involved competition and being outside has always been important to me.

Ironically, I discovered I had Parkinson's from running when I started having trouble with my foot locking up. Running has been a big part of my life. I ran in college, I ran after college, I broke records, and I made it to the Olympic trials. I have run all over the world.

I have always loved to compete, I didn't care what it was, whether it was Ping-Pong or croquet. Then when Parkinson's came along, I felt that my ability to do something athletic that allowed me to compete was taken away from me.

I have worked hard to battle Parkinson's. Exercise is the only thing that has proven to slow down the progress, no medicine does that, but exercise does. There is no cure, no cure in sight. I decided early on when it came to Parkinson's, I could be a contributor or a consumer.

What I mean is, as a contributor, I could work hard to be an active advocate for the cause by helping to find a cure and trying to make life better for others with Parkinson's. Or as a consumer, I could just sit back, make the most out of life, and reap the benefits of everyone who came before me.

Being a proactive kind of guy, I decided to be a difference maker. I travel all across the country and speak to groups about Parkinson's disease. Getting the word out is not easy for me because my mobility comes and goes, but it is important work.

I have been involved in lots of projects associated with Parkinson's, almost all of them with the help of the Parkinson's Foundation. I have found them to be an experienced and passionate organization. One reason is they are equally dedicated to making life better today, for people with Parkinson's, as they are to finding a cure. Knowing that they won't find a cure in my life time makes it really important to me to figure out how to make my life better today as I live with this disease.

I live in a neighborhood in Beaufort, SC, in a town called Haversham. It is unique because the town was developed with a concept called New Urbanism. It is designed to be a neighborhood like the old days, where everything is done and created so you will have lots of chances to bump into your neighbor.

I am a serious bike rider. I found cycling to be the best exercise mode for my Parkinson's. I have a road bike. I get out on the road and ride twenty-five to thirty miles at a stretch. On my way back home from my bike rides, I would go past the basketball court in our neighborhood and see these people setting up a net so they could play this game called pickleball.

Finally one day, I went up to them and asked if I could jump in and play. They said sure and when I started playing, I thought, "*Oh my gosh, this is awesome.*" Pickleball is unlike anything I have ever been around. I liked the pickleball atmosphere, so I started playing, and my wife started playing. I began thinking that pickleball is a fantastic sport for the right people with Parkinson's from a therapeutic standpoint, from an exercise standpoint, and from a mental health standpoint. It is the perfect game for all these reasons.

What a lot of people don't know is, the reason you get Parkinson's is that your brain doesn't produce enough dopamine. Dopamine does two things: it gives you the ability to move and it also creates your sense of well-being. Many people with Parkinson's isolate themselves. They don't go out; they don't leave home. There are cognitive and mental health issues.

Pickleball is incredibly social. Everyone is happy to be there, they are laughing, they are having fun, they want to know who is coming out next, and they are a very encouraging community of people. There is great emphasis on the social aspect of the game. You cannot discount the importance of being around other people. They have proven isolation makes Parkinson's disease worse and the disease will progress faster. You can't put a price tag on being around people who are laughing, having fun, and enjoying the fresh air.

From an exercise perspective, pickleball is not the best way to get the heart rate up, like biking can. But it involves and emphasizes hand–eye coordination as well as full-body movement, which is very important. While cycling might get my heart right up, it is not forcing me to time an incoming ball or precisely place a serve. Pickleball is a great complement to other forms of cardio exercise.

Here is the neatest thing: the more I learned about pickleball, the more I found out that the best pickleball players aren't running all over the court anyway. Being a banger is not what I would consider the most successful way to play pickleball. It's not that you can't bang it on occasion, but knowing where to be and how to get there safely without backpedaling is critical.

Being the kind of guy I am, I started wondering if we could teach people with Parkinson's how to play proper pickleball. For those who are able, it would open up a whole world of another sport that they didn't even realize existed.

One of my first steps toward being a contributor happened when I walked right into the Selkirk corporate office in Coeur D'Alene where my son lived at the time and asked if the CEOs Mike or Rob were around. Long story short: they have been very helpful spreading the word about the benefits of pickleball for people with Parkinson's.

I thought about Rock Steady Boxing, which is an organization where they train and certify coaches to improve the quality of life for people with Parkinson's through a non-contact boxing-based fitness program. I know these people pretty well. I figured I could use a similar model and get certified Parkinson's pickleball coaches. This way people will understand what Parkinson's disease is and the limitations that people with Parkinson's might have on the court.

I met Dr. Vanessa Hinson at a social gathering and found out she played pickleball. She is a neurologist with a specialty in movement disorders including Parkinson's disease and is the director of the program at the Medical University of South Carolina, which is a Center for Excellence for Parkinson's disease.

"Pickleball contains all of the elements that you need in an exercise program to be effectively helping your Parkinson's disease. Exercise is the most vital thing that a person with Parkinson's can do for themselves."

—Dr. Hinson

I shared my Parkinson's pickleball coaching idea with her and she was right on board. We are now working together, creating a whole curriculum to teach people with Parkinson's how to play pickleball and we are going to certify instructors all over the country.

We have our budget established, have the staff, and have the facility. It is going to happen. Ultimately, our vision is to have camps and tournaments for people with Parkinson's across the nation.

Pickleball has changed my life in so many ways: it allowed me to continue to compete and it gives me the platform to compete. I not only play and captain in local league, but I play in tournaments as well. I often play with another local guy who has Parkinson's. He used to be one of the top squash players in England and he is still really competitive.

I know this sounds terrible, but I love nothing more than we walk out on the court and our opponents see these guys with gray hair. They see that our mobility is not great and we might be tremoring.

"Then a lot of times I like to do a body bag and slam the ball against their body and then I apologize, of course," he laughs and smiles. "I knew they had underestimated us and it felt really good." He says playing tournaments and being able to compete feels as good as when he tried out for the Olympic running team.

Thinking Outside Of The Box

Brian and Valerie McCarthy

Rarely has there been a combo of a for-profit and not-for-profit venture, never one with as much heart and impact on its community as The Pickleball Club and the Play for Life Foundation. The founders, Brian and Valerie McCarthy, have combined their love for pickleball, their desire to help others, and their entrepreneurial spirit to create something truly special and the Sarasota, Florida, area has benefited from their vision.

Valerie and Rear Admiral Brian McCarthy have spent a lifetime building businesses and working to stay fit while guiding others to do the same. Brian, CEO of The Pickleball Club and chairman of the Play for Life Foundation, has decades of experience building organizations and developing commercial real estate. In addition to holding a degree in engineering and an MBA from Harvard, he is a combat veteran who served for 30 years in the U.S. Navy.

Valerie is the chief operating officer of The Pickleball Club and Executive Director of the Play for Life Foundation. Her career in physical fitness and operations included running her own fitness facility. As a lifelong athlete, she understands the connection between physical activity and well-being, and she walks the walk.

These two recognized the power of pickleball to change lives in positive ways and decided to use that as their platform. The Pickleball Club started in 2019, when they realized that the pickleball craze was taking over the nation. Florida comes with some unique weather issues, which makes playing pickleball outside on a regular basis a challenge, at best.

They did their research and determined that an indoor, private, amenity-based club was the best way to be a part of this movement. The first Pickleball Club opened in May 2023 in Lakewood Ranch, Florida, with a vision to build at least fifteen more locations in Florida. They currently have several hundred members who on average play three to four times a week. Valerie said the connections and changes she sees every day are truly heartwarming and inspiring.

The vision of The Pickleball Club is dedicated to improving lives, health, and longevity through the game of pickleball. They strive to exceed their members' expectations by making a difference every day in the lives of their community. The club focuses on the social aspect of the sport, as well as health and fitness and skill development. Since they feel connection is at the heart of pickleball, they provide social activities for their members and also a Pickles Café that encourages hanging out.

The Pickleball Club hosts events so members get the best of both worlds. "For a ladies night out event, thirty women showed up, not to play pickleball, but just to get together," Valerie said. "I believe pickleball is a catalyst for communication, and we really need that these days."

"One wonderful story involves a pair who came in to join together. As it turned out, they were a grandma and her grandnephew. I think that was really precious."

—Valerie

The Play for Life Foundation began in 2021 with a single vision to improve the mental and physical health of those most at risk by promoting a healthy and active lifestyle through pickleball. The foundation's mission is to introduce the sport to the community's youth, Veterans, and first responders. If you want to learn more about Play for Life Foundation, please visit www.p4l.org.

They developed a simple but ingenious idea called Club-N-Box, which contains nets, paddles, balls, and instructional material on how to play and set up a court. They provide a Club-N-Box to any qualified organization free of charge. They target at-risk youth to combat issues from sedentary activities like video games and the financial barriers to participation for team sports. They hope to help these youth avoid chronic illnesses associated with childhood obesity.

The Play for Life Foundation touched the lives of kids at Booker Elementary, an underserved school in the area. Through a grant, one of the teachers requested three Club-N-Boxes. They went out to the school with a couple of instructors, set up the nets, and the kids had a wonderful time playing. The teacher later shared that one boy was so violent in his hatred of PE and refusal to participate that they once had to call in the sheriff to restrain him. Now that he has fallen in love with pickleball, PE is no longer a problem and he is playing every day.

The foundation partners with high school athletic directors to encourage them to incorporate pickleball into their sports programs. The foundation even provides "train the trainer" instruction if needed.

Valerie would like to see schools develop teams. In the meantime, they started a league for high schoolers. These teams are using The Pickleball Club on Saturdays to play and practice. The season will end with a round robin tournament.

"We got a call after Hurricane Ian from a Sanibel Fire and Rescue responder asking if there was any way they could get a Club-N-Box because he thought that their first responders would benefit from it since everyone on the island had lost so much. We sent one to them and to the Captiva Station as well. This is one way that the Play for Life Foundation is really impacting people's lives and giving them something to smile about in spite of the surrounding disaster."

–Valerie

As a retired Navy officer and the daughter of a Marine, serving veterans is important to Brian and Valerie as a way of honoring their service and contributing to a more positive environment for veterans. Pickleball is easy to learn, more accessible than most activities for individuals with disabilities, and can be a great release for those with PTSD.

Play for Life provides pickleball and all its benefits to first responders seeking a physical outlet and a way to deal with the daily challenges of their jobs. In addition to Club-N-Box, they offer programs and special activities for firefighters, police officers, sheriff deputies, EMTs, and paramedics.

Valerie said, "One of the first responders shared with me that the guys really loved the camaraderie of being able to play pickleball at the station. They put the doors down at 6:00 and set up the nets and they play. If they exercise for thirty minutes per shift, they get a paid day off every three months. They have to stay fit, so it is an incentive to stay fit."

In less than two years, the foundation has given out six-ty Club-N-Boxes. They are in all the Boys and Girls Clubs in the Sarasota area and every Fire and Rescue Department in Manatee County. They have even received requests for a Club-N-Box from Massachusetts and Louisiana.

It is amazing what transformative changes a paddle, a ball, and a net can provide for people. Many say that when they get on the court, the whole outside world just disappears, and they are better able to cope with whatever curveball life or work has thrown at them.

"We are changing lives more than we ever imagined. There are some people who think we are a couple of bubbles off plumb, trying to do a brand-new business as well as a 501(3)(c) foundation. But Brian and I have always been committed to giving back to our community. We are really proud of what we have been able to accomplish and are looking forward to seeing our visons grow," Valerie said with excitement.

More Than Just The Money

Matt Gordon

My involvement with pickleball started on the business side. Brian McCarthy called me almost four years ago and said he wanted to talk about the concept of building indoor pickleball clubs. I thought it was a great business opportunity even though I knew nothing about the sport. Brian had been a client of mine 15 years ago. We became great friends and over the years stayed in touch.

We always wanted to do a project together, but the right one never came up at the right time until now. I am enjoying my role of acquiring investors for The Pickleball Club. Officially, I am a Wall Street mergers and acquisitions lawyer and I now serve as the Chief Financial Officer and Corporate Counsel for the McCarthy's The Pickleball Club ventures.

The Pickleball Club business has turned out to be a lot of fun. It is easy to get fired up every day when there are all of these extra societal benefits. We are helping to create a wonderful experience in our culture and our society.

I have very rarely been in a business where people randomly come up to you and say thank you. I had an investor in the club who happens to also be a member with his whole family. He sent me an email saying thanks for bringing us closer together as a family because of pickleball. It is a very special thing when you can make the world a better place and also improve your own personal financials.

It took about eighteen months after Brian's call before I started playing pickleball. I was an old, snooty tennis player and didn't see the need for pickleball in my life. One day while I was playing tennis, I got hurt, so I decided to try pickleball. I thought it was just going to be a recovery sport. I liked that it was possible to stand there and whack the ball and not have to run around too much, which is helpful if you are injured.

I started playing with four guys and we would put chalk lines on a basketball court in our town's public park. People would see us playing and be curious about pickleball. We would hand them a paddle and have them start out by practicing on the tennis court.

We went from five guys to 167 people in about two and a half years. I finally had some regular, adult-level socialization. I started playing once a week and it ended up where I was playing two to three times a week. I was less grumpy. I was drinking less on Friday nights so I could go to bed early and be fresh for the pickleball courts on Saturday morning.

We had winter groups, which was serious since this was a Westchester, New York, community, and afterwards we would go to a brew pub and have some beers. When women started joining the original group of guys, we didn't feel comfortable trash-talking around them, so we formed a group called "Shit-Talking Pickleball Dads." Although according to my daughter, who was thirteen at the time, our trash talk was really lame!

My son came home from the University of Michigan, and he and his friends wanted to play pickleball instead of having me make them breakfast, so I took them to the park and schooled them in the sport. Everyone wants to be part of the pickleball movement.

How does pickleball improve people's lives, especially those who are less advantaged? That is the whole premise behind the Play for Life Foundation. It provides opportunities for pickleball play for your entire life, which includes wellness, health, and mental well-being. There is no way to be in a bad mood when you play pickleball, even if you don't have the best game.

The news is always reporting about all the injuries from pickleball and how the players are keeping the orthopedists in business. This is true, but when you take a bunch of sedentary people and they start getting regular exercise playing pickleball, there will be injuries.

But the news fails to report how many heart attacks have been averted, how many cases of type 2 diabetes have been prevented, and how much early mortality has been avoided. I can't think of another thing that got more adults and senior citizens suddenly active while also improving loneliness and depression, leading to a better quality of life.

"So, you ask, 'What is our product at The Pickleball Club?' We are not selling pickleball play; we are selling the micro-community socialization opportunity in and around pickleball game play, and it is just what this world needs."

—Matt

"Julie and I were going to bed one night and I was almost asleep, but I heard a whispering sound: 'Build it and they will come.' After I heard it several times, I finally rolled over in bed, and there was Julie whispering this to me! Because of those sweet whispers in my ear, I knew we had to go forward."

—Rainer

Build It And They Will Come

Julie and Rainer Martens, founders of Pictona at Holly Hill, have created an incredible pickleball resource through private and public collaboration featuring forty-nine courts, including a championship court that can hold 1200 spectators.

But it is so much more than just a great place to play pickleball. It is an inclusive, educational oasis that has transformed a community and is making a lasting impression on players all over the country.

Holly Hill City Manager Joe Forte said he considers Pictona one of the greatest projects he has been involved in. "Holly Hill is being put on the map nationally among pickleball enthusiasts," he said. "We have people calling the Holly Hill Chamber asking for information about homes in the area because they want to relocate near Pictona."

When it comes to understanding how sports contribute to the human well-being, no one is more fitting to speak on the matter than Rainer and Julie Martens. Together they literally wrote a book on it. Rainer founded Human Kinetics, which has grown to be the largest publisher of sports, physical activity, and coaching resources in the world. Julie was Human Kinetics' first employee and an integral part of growing that business to the over 300-strong, employee-owned company it is today.

Rainer is also an internationally recognized sports psychologist, known for creating the American Sport Education Program. It is considered to be the most widely-employed coaching education program in the U.S. and has been used by over two million coaches. He has also authored several books, perhaps the most well-known being *Successful Coaching*, a best-selling coaching textbook.

Using pickleball as their vehicle for change, they have been able to capitalize on the incredible growth of the sport while keeping true to their lifelong mission of helping people to live more fulfilling lives through education, physical activity, and better nutrition.

"This has been a fun journey for us. I spent much of my professional academic and publishing career studying physical activity, practicing sports psychology, and publishing the results of my research. It was not always 'hands-on' work with individuals. Our experience with pickleball has lead us to actually get to work directly with people at our facility. We walk around and watch the players play every day and we get their suggestions and feedback. It's our observational test tube," said Rainer.

"The idea for Pictona was an evolution," Rainer said. "It wasn't something that we could see at the beginning. We were going to be happy to build eight to ten courts somewhere. Then we discovered the vacant park across the street from the city of Holly Hill, and the city manager and the mayor encouraged us to consider building some courts there."

"Our vision expanded because of their encouragement and the available land," Rainer said. "So, we decided to build twenty-four courts in our first phase. Once we were up and running, we were asked to host tournaments. But our members didn't have a place to play because the tournament took up all of the courts, so we decided to build another twenty-five courts and have one be a championship court that seats 1200."

The couple wanted to create an environment of health and well-being for everyone. They have a senior activity center with a large game room and adjacent recreation spaces for shuffleboard, croquet, cornhole, and golf putting that are free to the public.

"We did not set out to change the world. We were just looking to make more courts available, not only for us, but for all of the people in the greater Daytona area. How it ended up evolving was terrific."

—Julie

Julie was excited about how the age of members and visitors at Pictona has changed. Though they had mostly an older membership when they started, the age range has increased dramatically. They began with an average member age in the sixties and now the average age is in the early forties.

The Martens are eager to have people with special abilities play at their venue as well. "There is a special Olympic group that comes to the facility on a regular basis. They have a new group of individuals with Parkinson's disease starting up. There was a group of players in wheelchairs who played at our facility. Rainer and Julie want to see anybody and everybody playing pickleball.

They also offer exercise and educational classes to the community on a regular basis through their public and corporate partnerships. They have public gardens that they use to grow produce for The Kitchen, a restaurant on the premises.

Julie comments on why pickleball is so addictive and why she thinks people keep coming back to play. "I think that the nature of the sport is unique," Julie said. "People can go out for the first time, learn the basics, start to have fun and see what the sport holds for them. They can begin to challenge themselves to get better from the get-go."

"We see lots of happy people at our facility. We hear life-changing stories pretty frequently here, which reinforces our decision to have created this place."

—Rainer

"In tennis, you spend a lot of time trying to learn the basic skills so that you can enjoy the sport," she said, "and it takes a lot longer to get to a point where you're having fun. Pickleball offers that right off the bat. I think that is one of the reasons people keep coming back. They see where they can have fun today and where they can go tomorrow."

Rainer adds, "I think the pandemic contributed to the growth of pickleball. It was a safe activity and Pictona was available as a place to play. A number of people told us how important it was that they could get out of the house, engage in physical activity, and socialize with other people safely. I think that was a real big contribution of the sport to the welfare of the people going through the pandemic."

"It's been very rewarding to us to see all of the people having a good time at Pictona," Julie said. "This is not only our happy place but it's their happy place." At ages and seventy-four, Rainer and Julie see this as their legacy. "We helped design the place, we helped fund the place, and we help operate the place every day along with our terrific staff," Rainer said. "It's our dream come true that we will be able to leave behind when we are no longer here."

When asked if they continue to play and compete, Julie commented, "Having built Pictona, we can play whenever we want. We both still like competition. We tried for years to play together, but we don't anymore. It's funny, I think it is the only thing we don't do together competitively. We did win a couple of tournaments as partners, but we find the ride home a lot more enjoyable when we have different teammates.

Rainer brags on Julie and her pickleball prowess. "Last year the USA Pickleball Diamond Championship was held at Pictona and about 1200 players participated after first qualifying in a regional tournament," he said. Julie played in singles, women's doubles, and mixed doubles matches, and won gold in all three categories.

"That is the good news," Rainer jokes. "The bad news is that she wears those medals to bed and I can't sleep because they rattle all night long!"

Julie chimes in that Rainer won the men's doubles in the same tournament. Since then, he got his new knee and is about ready to get back on the courts.

"If you try your best to win, but also try to elevate your opponents so that they can do their best, you will find great enjoyment in any sport, including pickleball. I think maybe this sport is a little more social. People are enthused about it. I think over time pickleball will take its place alongside other more traditional sports. We are seeing rapid changes now due to the professionalization of it. I think you'll see it move into the schools more, in a big way. I think it will be an Olympic sport in a few years."

—Rainer

The Love Languages of Pickleball

Quality Time
Bringing friends together on the
pickleball court

Acts of Service
Teaching newbies how to play

Physical Touch
Bumping paddles after a good point

Words of Affirmation
Giving positive encouragement as a player

Gift Giving
Buying me the pickleball PJs that I wanted

Chapter 5

Our Hearts Belong to Pickleball

We were eager to find out why pickleball appeared to be more than just the latest sports fad. We felt that pickleball seemed to touch our hearts, and we wanted to know, "What is it about the sport that keeps us coming back to play?"

Everyone we asked mentioned that they would continue to play because it was fun and they liked the social aspect of the game. Close behind those two reasons were that playing pickleball was good exercise and a great way to meet new people. Many players loved the sport because it was easy to learn. Lots of folks said that it was an enjoyable way to spend time outdoors.

Some really loved the competition of the sport. Quite a few players said that it was easy to feel competent quickly. For many, it was a great way to spend time with their spouse, partner, or family. Pickleball was clearly quality time together for them.

All of these reasons emphasize the emotional aspect of pickleball and it fills your soul and leads to a yearning to return for more.

Their comments brought out some specific special points and made us smile.

- Playing pickleball makes them feel like a kid again.
- Pickleball is an outlet for things that ail you physically or emotionally.
- Pickleball is a thinking game and offers a mental challenge.
- Coaches love the rewarding feeling of helping people improve their game.
- Several women told us that playing pickleball kept them out of the kitchen—literally!

Bruce's Story

Pickleball breeds friendships. Of all the wonderful benefits pickleball gives us, none may be more pronounced than the friendships we gain. No matter at what level we play, beginner, intermediate, or competitive, it is incredible how many new friends we add to our growing list.

Consider this: almost everything outside of the actual game is about acquiring new friends. Sometimes it happens when we least expect it. Other times, we can't wait to say "Hi" and introduce ourselves. Friends are gained, friendships flourish, and life gets better. Pickleball makes it happen!

Often people ask me, "What is pickleball?" I never conclude until I tell them that pickleball is a gift. It's a gift because aside from the great exercise it offers, it also offers friendships.

Joann's Chilly Tale

During the first days of having our community outdoor courts, the weather was particularly cold. The pickleball community was about thirty people in all at that time. Many nights we played in parkas with wool hats and could see our breath because it was so cold. But we still continued to play every night. It was so cold that the balls would crack! We did not care; we just wanted to play.

Sonny's Story

My story is about as cliché as it comes. My wife and I retired, traveled for a year in an RV, and then settled into a "traditional" retirement life here in Crossville, Tennessee. We had moved from Long Island, New York, and we didn't know anybody. I felt kind of lost.

We explored Tennessee and did a lot of hiking and sightseeing, but I was still uneasy and, deep inside, unhappy with myself. I found I was becoming more isolated, physically lethargic, reclusive, sitting too much on my couch, and eating myself into obesity and declining health.

I used to own a home and always had something I needed to do around the house. Now we have a small condo and there wasn't much for me to do when we moved in. I felt displaced, with nowhere to be, nowhere to retreat, no projects that needed getting done, no purpose, and no schedule. I was sinking into depression, which is ironic since I couldn't wait to retire and "live life."

I remember praying and asking God for help. Shortly after, my wife suggested we take another walk around the community. It was then we were drawn to the constant thumping and banging sounds in the distance. Like hypnotized zombies, we followed the repetitive noise to see what all the "racquet" was about.

There, out in the open behind a maze of fences, were maybe fifty-sixty people of all shapes and sizes laughing and grunting, playing a unique and new-to-us game. We asked ourselves, "What is this pickleball?" Curious, we hesitantly signed up for a beginner's clinic. Personally, I didn't know if I was ready to give up being a couch "potato" to be a "pickle" ball player!

We met about twenty new people who instantly became twenty new friends, and together we all got hooked on this strange new game that I had heard almost nothing about until that day when we took a walk.

Together, my wife and I started training and playing seriously—or more like serious fun! Within four months, we formed close friendships, got back in shape, and lost a ton of weight. Now we are both in better shape and healthy. We're excited to get to the courts nearly every day, where little by little, we are getting to know everyone. We are thinking of taking road trips to play in tournaments.

I honestly believe God heard my prayers for help and pickleball was His answer. Pickleball definitely changed my life for the better, and I'm not apologizing for it either! Now all I have to say is: 0-0-start, game on! What are you waiting for?

In January of 2024, I weighed 170 pounds! I know I don't have the same muscle mass as my Navy days, but I do know that today I have nearly no stomach issues, no knee or back pains, no headaches, no shortness of breath, near normal blood pressure, and increased energy and mobility.

Best of all, I am off all cholesterol medications, have halved my blood pressure meds, and soon will be off them as well with my doctor's approval and monitoring. I can play over two hours of pickleball with little rest breaks. I am feeling better today than I have in the past ten years.

I share this because ten months ago, a Facebook friend posted something similar, and because of his post, I was encouraged to make these lifestyle changes through pickleball. I am passing my story forward in hopes that someone out there will be motivated enough to improve their physical well-being too. It's not easy, but then nothing worth having ever is!

Love At First Volley

Mark's Side of the Story

My pickleball journey began with my refusal to play the game because I thought it was for old folks. My community in Reno, where I live, had a temporary court set up in the street while our homes were being built. All we had were painted lines and a portable net. I didn't want to play, but all of the neighbors were playing, so I went and joined them. I felt it was more of a social event and a way to meet my new neighbors.

We would bring out our grills and barbeque something, have drinks, and enjoy the play of pickleball and the company of our neighbors. It was really neat, we had just the one court and sometimes we would have as many as twenty people.

After that first time, I was hooked and became addicted to playing the game. While the neighborhood play was a great bonding connection, I really wanted to progress and continue to get better. I knew I had to take my game beyond my home turf. Going outside my community was intimidating but I found people to be open and willing to play with me as the new guy. After my second year of playing and improving, I started hearing about tournaments and began competing at the 4.0 level all across the country.

Tournaments became fun outlets to test my skills and abilities and those of my partner as well as an opportunity for travel outside of my home base. I have made a number of destination trips involving pickleball tournaments from New York to Florida. It is that destination concept that took me to Tres Palapas, Mexico, where I met Ingrid, which changed my life forever.

Usually I play pickleball only in the summer. In the winter, I teach skiing at a ski resort. This particular year, I took a break from skiing to prepare for a tournament and to get away from the cold. Purely by random chance, Ingrid was also at Tres Palapas by herself, taking some training.

Now she is the light of my life and my significant other. We are planning a three-year cruise around the world and playing pickleball at many different locations. Ingrid is working with the cruise ship to get pickleball on board! I became certified to teach pickleball and hope I can arrange to give some pickleball lessons on the ship. Now, I have it all!

Love At First Volley

Ingrid's Version

Nine months ago, I started playing pickleball again when I was going through a bad breakup of a twelve-year civil union. It was either pickleball and the gym or homicide and overindulgence in alcohol and food. I had played ten years ago but took a bad fall because I didn't know what I was doing and stopped playing.

I discovered an incredible community at Pickleball Kingdom in Chandler, Arizona. They have outdoor courts indoors, so I was able to play during the day and well into the night, regardless of the sweltering 115 degree temperatures in Arizona. The community there was truly a bright star and a safe refuge when I was in an otherwise dim place.

Once the breakup was final, I decided I was going to really focus on playing pickleball and traveling solo while I figured out the next steps in my life. I took dozens of lessons and clinics. I went to Pictona in Daytona Beach, Florida, by myself and took the Scott Moore clinic, which was exceptional. I met some welcoming women and even joined the Singles Mingles Facebook group, although I didn't want to return to online dating.

I heard about Tres Palapas in Los Barrillos, Mexico, on Facebook and followed their group. It looked like great fun. Cabo isn't that far from Phoenix, so why not? I reached out and they put together a full week of clinics and classes for me. Tres Palapas was yet another community of welcoming pickleball players.

I was sitting at Tres Palapas on a Friday afternoon after a class had been cancelled due to extreme wind. I was waiting around because there was a Burger Night event there that evening. A gentleman named Mark walked in and just had the look and swagger of an advanced player. I am a 3.0 on a good day but getting exponentially better. Since the classes were cancelled, we decided to play in spite of the wind.

He played with me initially because, let's face it, there was no one else around. Later, the wind died down and more advanced players came to play. Mark was willing to continue to play with me, which I found amusing. After I had caused him to lose a couple of games, I insisted that he go and play with people in his league.

As the evening progressed and the music started playing, we moved on to the Burger Night activity. Mark hadn't reserved for the event, so I made sure he had something to eat and that we both had plenty of margaritas to drink.

Unfortunately, my ride back to our lodging wanted to leave early. Much to my surprise, Mark told someone during his game: "Tell her to wait; I'll take her back." I was glad to hear that because I truly didn't want to leave this great event . . . and those margaritas.

We spent the next two days together, playing pickleball, touring the beach, having drinks, and listening to local music. More advanced players were willing to play with me because Mark was willing to partner with me—I loved that feeling! He was cordial, articulate, and funny, and having someone from the opposite sex to talk to was so nice.

I had previously decided to reserve passage on a three-year cruise around the world (lifeatseacruises.com) looking to play pickleball all along the way. The cruise was to depart in November, so I certainly wasn't looking for any "relationship." I was determined nothing was going to stop me from going on this once-in-a-lifetime adventure.

Mark seemed nice enough and, like me, was physically fit, which was quite attractive. He said he was single, appeared to be emotionally available, and shared in my love of travel and pickleball. By the third day, I could tell we began to feel some sparks, but we were both leaving the next day. Besides, it was probably just an unexplored physical attraction, so "oh, well."

That Monday when my shuttle was unexpectedly cancelled, he offered to share his ride to the airport. I had no idea how I was going to get to the airport, so it was like a gift from God. As promised, he was reliable, on time, and took care of everything. There is something super sexy about a man who knows how to take charge.

We sat in the Amex lounge in Cabo, and simply enjoyed one another's company. We once again realized that we connected on so many levels, including our love of travel, our love of fine wine and champagne, and of course our love of pickleball. He also indicated that he had looked into my cruise and found the idea "intriguing."

Mark's flight left hours earlier than mine, and when he left, I realized that I really did miss him. "Get a grip and just let this go," I told myself. "He lives in Reno; you live in Phoenix. You probably won't see him again."

The next day, Mark reached out by phone, and we started talking daily. I actually looked forward to our conversations and waited for his call every evening. The connection was solidified over the next three weeks as we shared some of our most intimate secrets, desires, and plans for the rest of our lives. Mark became my safe haven.

I am an educated, older Black female who has previously dated interracially. Mark is a few years younger than I am, a successful, mostly-retired white man who has not dated interracially at all. However, he truly couldn't care less about that difference. He half-jokingly said, "I'll Google how to date a Black woman and find out what to do." Much like the pickleball community in general, neither of us see color, but the connections you make.

Mark and I agreed to meet in Las Vegas at a regional tournament he was playing in and the sparks flew there. The connection was indeed real, and during one of the hot days between matches, our eyes met, and I think we both just knew. We had fallen in love so quickly and so easily. The passion was off the charts!

We certainly have differences. Mark likes to read physical books; I like Audible. He likes rare meat; I like it medium. He is an avid skier and ski instructor; I prefer warm weather. But those differences are charming. What's important is that we are both the right people at the right time and place in our lives. We found each other when neither of us were looking, when we were emotionally and physically available, and now know that the quality of our lives is better together.

I am moving to Reno in the next couple of weeks to spend a whirlwind summer of fun in the sun, and of course play plenty of pickleball. I really have no reason to stay in Phoenix and a million reasons to go to Reno.

Mark and I plan to embark on the cruise together in November to discover those special places and enjoy our love of the pickleball. Mark is helping me improve my game tremendously. He is so patient and thoughtful (and did I mention sexy as hell?). He is truly my life partner. He and I became "we" all because of pickleball!

Not Just In The U.S.A.

Patrick's Story

Think the pickleball craze is only in the United States? Meet Patrick Batty, whose passion for pickleball changed his life and the lives of his fellow Canadians.

His story starts with his family. Patrick and his wife, Bonita, have been married 50 years with a daughter, son, and grandson. They live in southern Ontario, Canada, where Bonita was a teacher and Patrick worked as a software executive. During the pandemic, Patrick noticed something had changed with his wife's personality, and eventually she was diagnosed with Alzheimer's.

They were able to take a trip to Cuba in December of 2022, but the travel was difficult for Bonita and made her symptoms worse. Shortly thereafter, she ended up in the hospital. Patrick became depressed and lonely without her at home as her disease progressed.

In March 2023, he made up his mind to do something to help himself find happiness and reach out to others. Patrick was athletic, and having played tennis and squash in the past, he decided to try pickleball. By the second time, he was hooked. He admits to having an obsessive personality, and soon he was playing five days a week. "Pickleball is an easy game to play and a hard game to play well," Patrick said.

His town had very few facilities for pickleball, especially if you weren't a senior. There were only two outdoor courts in his town of 150,000 people. Being a go-getter, he saw the need and started the nonprofit Cambridge Pickleball Club. They started with sixty members and grew to 160 by November 2023.

From the beginning, Patrick charged just enough to cover the expenses of running the club and the rent on the facilities they used. Once the club was up and running, some of the new members asked about having lessons. So, Patrick took a forty-hour coach training course sponsored by Pickleball Canada and started offering a two-hour "introduction to pickleball" class.

When Patrick noticed there was no news site devoted to pickleball in Canada, he started *Pickleball Today* in 2023. It is now Canada's national pickleball news source with a wealth of information about the latest happenings in pickleball communities in Canada.

In August 2023, the Canadian National Professional Pickleball League (CNPL) was born with the mission of producing the highest level of competition and compensation for professional Canadian pickleball players. The league is committed to growing the sport across Canada, fostering a sense of community, competition, and camaraderie. The Canadian Professional Pickleball League now has an official partnership with *Pickleball Today.*

"It's great to know that we have the support of local media outlets, but with a partnership like this, we are able to get dedicated coverage by an outlet that truly understands this sport and what is valuable to its Canadian fans," said CNPL Commissioner Mike McAninch.

Patrick responded, "The Canadian National Pickleball League has provided a fantastic team-based platform for professional pickleball in Canada. We love their concept and execution. They have the best competitive professionals from across the country and are giving them a marvelous and rewarding competition, as well as providing fantastic sporting entertainment to the fans in attendance at their exciting events."

Love, Marriage, And Pickleball

Doug and Mindy

You never know whom you will meet at camp—maybe even your future spouse!

In 2018, Mindy travelled from Fort Wayne, Indiana, to Suncoast Montreat Strategic Pickleball Camp at Black Mountain, North Carolina, with some friends from Kentucky whom she met on the pickleball tournament circuit. Doug came from Lexington, Kentucky, to use his pickleball camp gift certificate, and they ended up at the same pickleball camp. They became casual acquaintances that year.

Mindy and Doug both returned to Suncoast Pickleball Camp in 2019. This time, they were in the same group and got to spend time together each day. The more they talked, the more their interest in each other grew. Turns out they were both in the health care field. Mindy was a family medicine nurse practitioner and Doug was a respiratory therapist. They both had three children from a previous marriage. To top it off, they both liked to eat around the outside of their plate first.

As their relationship continued to blossom, they stayed in touch on the phone and by visiting each other. By 2021, Mindy quit the health care business and became a pickleball instructor. Doug continued his job but became a pickleball camp helper so they could spend more time together.

In May 2023 at the Lake Susan bench at Montreat, Doug proposed and they shared their first kiss. A few months later, they celebrated their relationship by getting married at Montreat. Their ceremony was officiated by Pastor Bob White, a pickleball instructor and Baptist preacher who got ordained in North Carolina just for the occasion.

Family and friends enjoyed this unique ceremony on Court 16 with an aisle made up of two pickleball nets placed lengthwise. As the newly married bride and groom processioned off the court, the wedding guests formed an arch with pickleball paddles. Mindy and Doug walked under this creative and fitting walkway as husband and wife. Afterward, everyone continued the festivities at a reception at Phil's BBQ in Black Mountain.

Their honeymoon was spent at Montreat teaching and assisting at the Suncoast Pickleball Camp that began the next day. For them, it was the perfect way to start their lives together as a married couple.

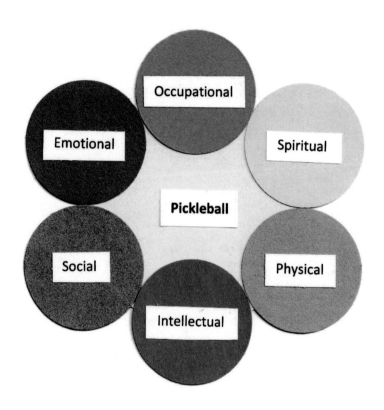

Chapter 6

Pickleball Is Wellness

Wellness is a multifaceted concept for assessing overall health and well-being. Bill Hettler, co-founder of the National Wellness Institute, created a model identifying six dimensions of wellness. Part of the success of pickleball and why it makes us feel so good is that it can enhance all six dimensions: physical, emotional, intellectual, spiritual, social, and occupational.

Physical Wellness

Physical wellness centers around health and fitness activities that support bodily health. Any sport or physical activity supports stamina, muscle tone, and strength while burning calories and improving lung capacity and blood flow. Pickleball also increases hand–eye coordination and improves hand speed, grip strength, and reaction time.

Multiple research studies have shown that grip strength can serve as a strong predictor of mortality and a vital health indicator of how a person is aging. In his 2022 study of 1,275 men and women, Dr. Mark Peterson found that those with weak grip strength showed signs of accelerated aging of their DNA.[2] Their genes appeared to be growing older faster than those of people with greater grip strength!

Grip strength has proven to have a positive effect on performance in sports like pickleball that use handheld equipment.[3] Activities involving weight-bearing and resistance improve muscle mass, which impacts grip strength and thus overall fitness.

Almost everyone said they benefited physically from playing pickleball. The bottom line: don't stop being physically active!

Pickleball Saved My Life

Jan P's Story

On Friday April 12, 2019, I played pickleball in the morning at the House of Pickleball, went to Chipotle in Wilmington for my favorite lunch, and then went to an early afternoon movie.

Toward the end of the movie, I started having a recurring cold sweat and experienced an off feeling. These were the same symptoms that I had the night before. I had no chest pain, no elephant sitting on my chest, but I felt that something was just not right.

To make a long story short, I decided to drive myself to the hospital to see if I was having a heart attack. I called my wife, who happened to be in Wilmington, and she met me at the Emergency Department. It turns out that I was having what is known as a "Widow Maker" event with four blocked arteries to my heart. The surgeon told me that I would have been dead in a week if I had not come to the hospital.

The odd thing was that I could play pickleball with no problem, could climb stairs with no problem, and I was never winded. The question was, "Why didn't I suffer from these symptoms?" The answer was pickleball.

The doctor said that pickleball had saved my life. The healthy part of my heart and my expanded lung capacity enabled me to be active and overcome the blockages. I joined the HOP in September 2018. The HOP was a perfect place for me to play with its multi-layered surfaces easing my achy knees from playing on outdoor hard surfaces, sweet air-conditioning, no annoying wind, and no dastardly sun. It was if I had died and gone to heaven (pun intended).

On top of those benefits, the HOP felt like a welcoming community. My wife and I have gotten to meet so many people from various developments and towns. We have met people with different and similar past jobs and life experiences. We have developed many close friendships, which led to dining out and visiting each other's homes. We have found a community that celebrates the highs of life and is supportive in more troubling times. What more could you want?

Pickleball truly enhances the body, the mind, and the spirit. My body survived in spite of my serious heart blockage, and I even lost sixty pounds. The mind is engaged in pickleball as the perfect Alzheimer's test, "What is the score and who the hell is serving?"

The spirit is touched by a community where males and females, young and old can play together (even though the young can get and recover from our older player "kill shots" so much more easily, the bastards), as well as the competitive aspect of the game playing with other people of similar skill sets and intensity. What's great is that no matter if you were a jock in high school or college, or if you were the kind of person who was picked last in gym class, you can find people that match your abilities and attitude. Nobody has to be left out.

Some people are concerned that when they start playing, they will get hurt. We all know that as we age, we can be injured walking on a flat surface (my wife will be happy to demonstrate that skill for you), getting out of bed, or getting off the couch.

The beauty of pickleball is that your body gets your muscles into shape, which can help your joints and reduce the effect of all those desserts that we crave by toning up. Endorphins released through exercise help us take less of those happy drinks and pills. Hell, even picking up those damn pickleballs six thousand times will replace the old stomach crunches we used to be able to do. You can once again touch your toes.

Pickleball also serves a great early warning system to test hearing. How many of us have heard from our opponents "I can't hear the score!" Ah . . . the challenges of pickleball.

The Schalins: Role Models for Successful Aging Through Pickleball

Beverly and Earl Schalin, a couple in their nineties, are using pickleball to prove that age is just a number!

After their retirement and relocation to Sun Lakes, Arizona, former competitive tennis players Earl and Beverly discovered pickleball. The sport was gentler on their bodies, and they relished the ceaseless action. Beverly had recently undergone rotator cuff surgery, and Earl had been struggling with back issues. Gradually, they played less tennis and more pickleball.

Before long, they were participating in and winning pickleball competitions. They had their inaugural teaching experience after volunteering to host a series of introductory clinics.

During their time in Arizona, they estimate that they taught over 400 people the art and skills of pickleball. When they relocated to San Diego, the people at Covenant Living at Mount Miguel quickly discovered they had pickleball champions in their midst and asked the Schalins to teach the game to the other residents and their families.

Many of the people they instruct possess some familiarity with tennis, but tennis demands a protracted learning curve and an even lengthier path to competitiveness. With pickleball, they can impart the essentials in fifteen to twenty minutes. Those who have played Ping-Pong hit balls back and forth right away. They may not be following all the rules or tracking the score, but they keep the ball in play for two, three, or four hits. The expression on their faces when they realize they are actually mastering the skills of pickleball is something to behold.

The Schalins now adhere to some modified rules to ensure the game is safe for older players. One such rule is "no lobbing." They wanted to avoid situations where individuals have to retreat backwards, since that poses a risk of falling. They also refrain from charging up to the net. Earl says they "mosey" instead.

These modifications keep pickleball accessible to people of all ages and abilities. The Schalins talk with many people who are ambulatory but have knee issues and can't pivot sideways. Beverly encourages them to come and observe rather than just assuming they can't do it. Using this approach, now many of their friends with previous knee replacements are out playing pickleball. The Schalins and their friends are shining examples that pickleball is possible for nearly everyone.

Walt's Story

I often say that pickleball helped save my life. Maybe that is a bit of an exaggeration, but so is my self-proclaimed title of "champion of the world!" About three years ago, I was playing pickleball three times a week and walking three or four miles on the days that I didn't play pickleball. I had just made a comment to a friend that I was probably in the best shape of my life, except for more than a few extra pounds.

The next day during a routine endoscopy, the doctor found a tumor in my esophagus that turned out to be cancerous. During the first four or six weeks of weekly chemotherapy and daily radiation treatments, I was able to maintain a normal pickleball schedule. This helped me physically to stay active and get emotional support from the other players.

Pickleball gave me something to look forward to and helped me keep a positive healing attitude. After a recovery period to regain my strength, I underwent a procedure to remove my esophagus and reform my stomach into a pathway from my mouth to my stomach.

I showed up for the surgery wearing my t-shirt, which had a stick figure with a cast and bandages that said, "Tell me, doc, can I play Pickleball tomorrow?" Then I went into surgery with a head gear that said "Best Day Ever" as the surgery would remove that last traces of cancer.

The surgeon, staff, and my supportive family were amazing, and I was able to leave the ICU after eight days instead of the usual eleven to twelve days. It was a tough few days, but I believe that my positive attitude, endurance from playing pickleball, and all the prayers, cards, and encouraging comments from family and friends helped me recover more quickly.

To be able to play pickleball again gave me the incentive to do my rehabilitation routines. It took me about four months to recover enough to play the game that I love. I was a little lighter and a bit weaker but still able to enjoy the game and the camaraderie.

Emotional Wellness

Emotional wellness is an awareness, understanding, and acceptance of our feelings and our ability to manage effectively through challenges and change. In the game of pickleball, this translates into teamwork and good sportsmanship.

For example, pickleball games move quickly and the game momentum can change on a dime. Communication with one's partner needs to be efficient and effective. This becomes even more important when your team falls behind. Court position, setting up the point, and stacking all require constant communication while working in tandem with your partner. Often the outcome of the game will depend more on partner connections than the actual skill of the players.

Pickleball culture is one of compliments and support. Often we hear "great shot" and "good try," even for the opposing team, and applaud each other by tapping our paddle tips together after a great shot. At the end of a game, it is customary for all players to come to the net, tap paddles, and say "good game." It adds positivity to the entire game and strengthens emotional wellness.

Compassion In Competition

Jesse's Story

I was playing singles at the U.S. Open in the pro division. I won two out of my first three matches and started to have painful leg cramps due to the heat and extreme exertion. Since the cramping started before I played Dave G. in my fourth match, I knew I would need to use up my timeouts to be able to continue playing in the heat.

After I took my second timeout, Dave saw that I was struggling and called two timeouts for me, so I could recover to compete even though he was winning. I was very grateful, and to my amusement, I watched Dave order and chug a beer while I ate some mustard and stretched my legs. He proceeded to beat me in the game. I thanked him for his compassion while we both had a laugh about the beer.

Intellectual Wellness

Intellectual wellness encourages us to find ways to expand our knowledge and skills while keeping our minds sharp. This lifelong learning can be applied to personal goals, group interactions, and community involvement, which are all components of pickleball. Continuous learning is beneficial to the mind and body.

Pickleball is a relatively new and unique sport for most people. We are challenged to learn the basics of the game and translate those concepts and skills into actions on the court. We then move on to the next level and continue to expand our knowledge and skills.

After we have become proficient, we get to the real brain work of the "chess match" of pickleball, which keeps our brains forming new connections. Once you master your shot selections and placement, the next step is planning a series of shots and positioning to set up for your kill shot. Pickleball at this intensity allows your brain to function at the highest level.

Social Wellness

Social wellness involves building healthy, nurturing, and supportive relationships as well as fostering genuine connections with those around you. Surrounding yourself with positive social networks increases your self-esteem. Having good social wellness is critical to building emotional resilience.

Pickleball knocks it out of the park for social wellness on so many levels. Online pickleball communities form social connections through platforms like TeamReach and WhatsApp. These apps are used for communicating with other pickleball players in your area to set up games, ask questions about shots, rules, equipment, or any other need-to-know pickleball topics.

Each "group" is a community in itself, which is social networking at its best. Often all you have to do is ask someone you met to put you in their "group" and instantly you are a part of that community. This is a great way to spread the love for the game.

Open play is another unique and highly social aspect of pickleball. Wherever pickleball is played, there will be open play, which is just like it sounds: people of any age or skill level will come together and play for a designated period of time, rotating to games with different players. There is a tremendous amount of group interaction and cooperation and community bonding that is fostered through open pickleball.

As if that wasn't enough, U.S.A. Pickleball is an organization created for the purpose of bringing pickleball into people's lives. They have developed a network of pickleball ambassadors. They are all volunteers, whose sole purpose is to introduce pickleball to people, teach them how to play, create playing opportunities within their communities, and connect players with one another.

The labor of love that goes into being a pickleball ambassador is rewarded by passing along the joy for the sport. They bring the game to schools, community centers, senior centers, and underserved communities. To find your ambassador, go to usapickleball.org. The ambassador program is under the "Get Involved" tab. Put in the name of your town and see who the pickleball ambassador is in your area.

Spiritual Wellness

Spiritual wellness recognizes our purpose for human existence, seeking respect and meaning in one's life. Not as lofty as the global "meaning of life," pickleball has some spiritual significance for many.

For those playing pickleball outdoors, they are also communing with nature and enjoying the beauty of the universe. Some would suggest there should be pickleball at places of worship!

The stories we received of how pickleball changed people's lives by giving them more meaning and purpose, connection to others, and better physical health show a strong basis for spiritual wellness.

Occupational Wellness

Occupational wellness allows you to explore various career options and encourages you to pursue the opportunities you most enjoy. This dimension of wellness recognizes the importance of satisfaction, enrichment, and meaning through work. The ability to achieve a balance between work and leisure in a way that promotes health provides a sense of personal satisfaction, and is financially rewarding, resulting in occupational wellness.

The possibilities to create, work, and benefit financially from pickleball are significant. People are changing careers to be part of the fun of pickleball and training to be coaches and professionals, creating pickleball clubs and camps. With the increasing popularity of pickleball comes a wealth of business opportunities available to those who are willing to take the leap.

Pickleball businesses started out meeting the basic needs of players with equipment, apparel, and places to learn and to play. Over the past several years, we have seen pickleball businesses boom in more niche areas, such as pickleball jewelry, novelty t-shirts, pickleball-themed party goods, and bars and restaurants associated with pickleball courts.

Pickleball Corporate Team Building

Christine and Peter Burrows

Peter and I first played pickleball in a friend's backyard in the summer of 2015. They had no clue about the rules, so we had a blast charging the net and putting balls away. When we returned the next summer and were told about "the kitchen," the game seemed a lot harder.

Eventually, we found ourselves sampling the sport again in North Carolina on local courts in Carolina Beach, and it's now become our favorite activity. We play as often as we can and try to play wherever we go to meet new people.

Since we are contemplating retirement, we started wondering how we could bring our professional talents to the pickleball courts. Using a career coaching technique called ikigai that explores the intersection between what you love, what you are great at, what you believe the world needs, and what you can get paid for, we landed on the idea of using pickleball to help corporate teams become better at communication, collaboration, and strategizing. We combined our love of the sport, desire to introduce it to others, and professional coaching experiences to develop a curriculum for teambuilding on the courts.

PickleBall Corporate Building (www.pb-cb.com) offers work teams the opportunity to learn and play pickleball while exploring some simple metaphors between how people play and how they work. Our "pickle-isms" are short drills that focus on a single aspect of the sport that also happen to align with some aspect of collegiality.

For instance, "Paddles Up" is a volley drill where players keep their paddles up to be most prepared to receive the ball. They also develop trust in their partner who conveys their readiness as well. This translates into the workspace where team members want their colleagues to show up ready to work.

"OURS" is a communication drill where players must call the ball each time, indicating to their partner that they will hit the ball or they expect them to take it. Much like in the workplace, communication and accountability are keys to successful teaming.

Our goal is not to make great pickleball players out of our clients, but to share our love of the sport while helping them reflect a little bit on how they relate as work teammates. The pickleball court provides a relatively easy way to have fun and invest in building stronger work teams at the same time.

The bottom line is that being involved in the sport of pickleball contributes to all dimensions of wellness, which directly contributes to our overall well-being, happiness, and longevity. So, play on!

Pickleball Rap
by ChatGPT

Let me tell you 'bout a game that's taking over the court
It's called pickleball, and it's a real sport
Smaller than tennis, but bigger than Ping-Pong
And once you start playing, you can't go wrong

Pickleball, pickleball, it's the game of the year
Grab a paddle, hit the ball, and let's all cheer
It's a cross between tennis, badminton, and fun
So come on, everybody, it's "Game on"

You don't need to be an athlete to be good at this game
Just a little skill and some strategy,
And you'll be in the hall of fame
It's a game for all ages, every woman and man
So come on, let's play, and let's make a stand

You might think it's easy, but it's harder than it looks
You gotta be quick and nimble, like a fish on a hook
The ball can come at you fast, so you gotta be alert
But when you hit that perfect shot, it's worth all the work

Pickleball, pickleball, it's the game of the year
Grab a paddle, hit the ball, and let's all cheer
It's a cross between tennis, badminton, and fun
So come on, everybody, it's "Game on"

So that's my rap about pickleball,
The game that's all the rage
Come on, let's go play, and let's engage
It's a game that's fun and inclusive, and it's here to stay
So grab a paddle, hit the ball, and let's all play!

IT AIN'T COMIN' BACK
TRACK IN AND OUT ⚙ HIGH & HARD
WEIGHT TRANSFER ON ALL SHOTS
ALL DAY ⚙ PUSH 'EM BACK....KEEP 'EM BACK
MAKE LIFE DIFFICULT TO DROP ⚙ IT'S A STROKE NOT A POKE
GROWL, GRUNT, EXHALE, ALWAYS BE LOOKING MOVE AS AN OCEAN WAVE
⚙ **DON'T MISS THE COURT & HOLD YOUR GROUND**
WITH THE WIND DON'T LOB ⚙ STAY BALANCED ⚙ QUICK-QUICK-SLOW
PATIENCE, CHOOSE WISELY, HOG THE MIDDLE, SCURRY ⚙
DON'T FLINCH ⚙ **KEEP THE BALL IN PLAY DROP-STOP-POP**
VARY DEPTH, PACE & SPIN ⚙ SERVE DEEP, RETURN DEEP & STAY SQUARE
BUTT DOWN, CHEST UP, PADDLE UP ⚙ **MAKE THEM PAY**
⚙ 'EARN' THE NET, CLEAR THE NET, DO SOMETHING DIFFERENT
LOW & SLOW LOOK TO POACH ATTACK ⚙
FOCUS, SETTLE ⚙ **GLIDE DON'T HOP**
LIMIT THE BACKSWING TRIANGULATION
RESPECT THE NET

DEB'S MANTRAS

Credit: Deb Harrison, pickleball teacher and coach.
She can be contacted at picklepongdeb.com

Chapter 7

Pickleball Pearls Of Wisdom

Pickleball culture includes helping others learn to play and improve. We asked our pickleball public what advice they would give to their fellow pickleballers and newbies. Some thoughts were instructional and others motivational. Several spoke to the joy and camaraderie the game fosters, and some were just plain amusing!

- Have fun! Enjoy! Remember, fun is the top goal.
- Try to learn from those who are better than you and thank them.
- Be a great partner no matter what level they are or how wellor badly they are playing.
- Be nice!
- Don't be afraid to try pickleball by yourself; you will be welcomed.
- Let the bad shots go, smile, reset your attitude and have fun—it's just a game.
- Be grateful to be out there playing.
- There are many people willing to help you improve; just ask.
- Be patient.
- The improvement journey is not linear; keep building on your knowledge and skills.

- It is easy to become an average player but hard to master the skills needed to be an advanced player.
- Don't get discouraged; keep drilling.
- There will be good days and bad days.
- Don't allow a score of 1–10 to deter you from thinking the game is over.
- Don't be cocky and think that a score of 10–1 is a sure win.
- Go into the game with a plan and coach yourself beforehand.
- Keep playing and vary your fellow players.
- When you start playing, pick one or two people to teach you and block out everyone else.
- Hit it where they aren't!
- Hit the ball with the paddle in front of your body and watch the ball until it leaves your paddle.
- Learn the third shot drop, learn positioning on the court, and learn how to dink.
- Move your feet.
- Take your time and let your opponent make the mistakes.
- Be like taffy and stretch before playing.
- Keep that ball low and slow.
- Placement over power all day long.
- Play like every shot is coming back.
- Stop with the death grip on the paddle handle.
- Master the cross court shot.
- Down the middle solves the riddle.
- Shoulder high, let it fly!
- Get up to the net—getting to the kitchen line is a goal but not a race.
- Don't run backwards.

- Talk to your partner—teamwork makes the dream work.
- Play smarter, not harder.
- When the score is 2-2-2, do a ballet twirl before the serve.
- When I put my paddle up to go for a ball and change my mind, I bring my paddle down quickly and say "Teacher, I forgot the answer!"
- When my partner or I make an amazing shot, I say "Wish I could bottle that and put a cork on it!"

We also looked into what some coaches and pros had to say about the special skills they bring to the court and the best way to improve your game.

"My two best pieces of advice are for players to put balance above all else and don't rush to the kitchen. Too often players are told to get up to the kitchen right away and that most points are won at the kitchen. When players prioritize getting to the kitchen above getting balanced in an athletic stance, they sacrifice more than they gain. With balance as a priority, it is easier to create muscle memory and consistency with your shots."

—Coach Jesse

"Previous years of playing tennis, racquetball, and high-level Ping-Pong gave me a leg up on my pickleball game. Also, I was an offensive outside hitter/spiker in volleyball, so I have a good overhead kill shot. I have been blessed with outstanding health for a 65-year-old. I am retired, so I have plenty of time to drill and play to improve my game. I have the ability to always keep the competitive aspect of the game in balance with the fun aspect, so I never become frustrated, negative, or get 'down' on myself and never ever get 'down' on my partner or blame them for our team's underperformance."

—Coach Steve

Anna Leigh Waters

Professional Player

At age seventeen, Anna Leigh Waters is the women's number one pickleball player.

Anna Leigh started out playing tennis and soccer. Her grandfather invited her mom and her to play pickleball when they evacuated their home in Florida after Hurricane Irma in 2017. They both fell in love with the game and began playing together.

Soon, they were competing in tournaments and being recognized for their savvy and aggressive playing style. The two pioneered a new playing style of banging and ripping on the court, muscling their way through points rather than patiently dinking and waiting for their opponents to make a mistake. Anna Leigh credits her mom for giving the game a more fast-paced competitive edge.

Part of their success as a doubles team comes from their ability to sense where the other one is going to be on the court. Now that her mom is her coach, she usually partners with Anna Bright or Catherine Parenteau for doubles and with Ben Johns for mixed doubles. Anna Bright says Anna Leigh is feisty and an absolute beast on the court.

Anna Leigh's mental strength and competitive edge helped launch her to the top of her game. She often turns to Coach Mom for a "mental tune-up session" and reminds herself that "pressure is a privilege." Giving yourself grace can be tough because the brain generates thousands of often unhelpful and negative thoughts each day. Actively switching gears to positive thoughts has helped her succeed.

When Anna Leigh feels the pressure inching closer on the court and needs to climb out of the hole, she calls a time-out and talks to herself. She takes a deep breath, analyzes her strategy, and focuses on her mindset. This helps to center her, often snapping her back into the game to make a comeback.

"When you're in the hole, you have to stay positive because your opponent is trying to beat you, and if you're trying to beat yourself too, then that's two against one. Believe in your shots. Believe in your game and what you've done."

—Anna Leigh Waters

Ben Johns

Professional Player

Ben Johns was sixteen in 2016 when he picked up a paddle for the first time on his family's annual winter pilgrimage to Florida. In 2019, he became the first male professional to win a Triple Crown (a gold medal in singles, doubles, and mixed doubles).

As of 2024, he is the world's number one men's pickleball player, securing his 100th gold medal on the Professional Pickleball Association tour at just twenty-four years old. At the start of 2020, Johns held a staggering 108th match, winning streak in singles, lasting over a year of tournament play. He also excelled in both men's and mixed doubles.

Johns added a dimension of athleticism and thinking to the sport. As he spent time with better players, he took notice of everything he liked and disliked about their games. Johns acknowledges that, from the start, he seemed to have an edge that other beginning players did not. "I was very much a visual person who would watch other things, imitate them, and then adapt from there," he said.

He turned each practice into a research-and-development session, building an arsenal of shots, including many that no one had ever seen. "Even when not playing well, he'll still outmaneuver you," Hannah Johns, one of Ben's six siblings and a commentator for the sport, said of her brother. "He'll out-strategize you. He's thinking six, seven shots ahead."

This sentiment is echoed by Thomas Shields, founder of *The Dink* website. He also said of Johns, "When I've played with him, I've noticed that just from an athletic perspective, his hands are insanely fast. His reflexes are unbelievable. You'll nail the ball at him, to the side of him, you'll have a whole open court, you're going to hit a winner, and somehow he's able to get it back over."

Ben believes that experience and confidence, rather than overt self-assurance, are key to mental toughness in sports. He emphasizes the importance of believing in one's ability to win and learning from each competition. Ben identifies his nonchalant attitude as both a strength and an area for improvement.

He reminds us not to miss opportunities to attack. He believes in the philosophy of not looking back. He views losses as learning opportunities, urging young athletes not to dwell on defeats.

Ben's primary advice for aspiring athletes is to enjoy the journey toward their goals. He stresses the importance of finding joy in training. He advises athletes to practice their weaknesses and enjoy group learning environments like pickleball retreats.

"It turns out that bending your knees in pickleball is just straight magic."

—Ben

Tyson McGuffin

Professional Player

Tyson McGuffin is one of the top-ranked male pickleball players in the world. He is a five-time Grand Slam Champion and a four-time National Champion known for his speed, physicality, serve, forehand, and determination. Forehand speed-up with a forehand clean-up is his favorite shot. His ability to change the pace of the game and keep his opponents off-balance is what sets him apart.

The key, according to Tyson, is "less is more." No need to cream the ball. He says you should attack the ball when you have great BPS.

What is BPS?

Balance — Be sure to have a good center of gravity without moving forward or backwards too much.

Position — It's often a bad time to attack when you or your partner has been pulled out wide. Most attacks don't win the point outright, so wait and attack when both you and your partner can cover the counterattack shot.

Strike Zone — When the ball is in your green zone (above the waist) you have the "green light." In the yellow zone (knees to waist) you should use caution. It's rare that you should want to attack from the red zone (below the knees), though one effective red zone shot is a top spin lob from the kitchen when you have good balance and position. You likely want to attack every ball in your green zone (or dodging them if they are going out) and play defense with most balls hit to your red zone. The yellow zone is more of the grey area and depends on skill level and the difficulty of the shot.

Anna Bright
Professional Player

Before pickleball, Anna Bright played on the U.C. Berkeley women's varsity tennis team and reached a career-high ranking of thirteenth in the country. Originally from Fort Worth, Texas, she began playing pickleball with her parents in October 2021, worked for DUPR (Dynamic Universal Pickleball Rating) for a brief time, and is now a full-time pro. Anna is ranked fourth in women's singles, third in women's doubles, and tenth in mixed doubles.

She brings passion and fire to every game she plays, and her competitive spirit is contagious. Her ability to perform under pressure and her strategic gameplay make her a formidable opponent to anyone on the court.

Anna's shot placement is a key aspect of her game. She has mastered the art of hitting shots to specific areas of the court, forcing her opponents into difficult positions. By consistently aiming for the corners and sidelines, she maximizes her chances of winning points. Anna's control over the ball enables her to execute drop shots, lobs, and powerful drives with precision.

Anna's advice to improve your game is to watch a lot of pickleball, play with players who are better than you, and believe you can do hard things.

Tina Lum is a professional pickleball player in the National Pickleball League. A 5.0 gold medalist with numerous trips to nationals under her belt, she was drafted by the Austin Ignite team in their inaugural 2023 season.

Before discovering her pickleball passion, she was an accomplished competitive tennis and paddle tennis player. While playing platform tennis, she tore her ACL. After her recovery, her paddle tennis partner suggested pickleball, which she felt would be easy for Tina to learn and easier on her knee.

Tina recalls, "My first time was at the Ridgefield rec center. I got a random paddle at Dick's. I had no idea what I was buying and just took the advice of the salesperson. I started playing and my first impression was, "WOW! I think I became almost instantly addicted."

"Like all the sports I play, I totally dive in, like a dog to a ball, and so I started playing a ton of pickleball. Since there were no pickleball courts nearby, I had to drive about forty-five minutes to play. I loved my new sport and my new group of friends. I became obsessed with wanting to get better and better and wanting to compete."

She was so into the competitive aspect of the sport that she got her whole family involved. "Every time we take a family vacation, we find a place that has a tournament," she said.

In 2022, Tina got involved with the National Pickleball League, a professional league for players aged fifty and older. Pickleball was the first sport to have a professional league devoted to older players. She was drafted onto a team of eighteen players she had never met.

"The team feel compared to just you and your partner at a tournament was just that much more exciting," Tina said.

"You cheered for your team, and you cheered for yourself. There was a lot of camaraderie. It was also competitive, and all of the emotions of competing were involved in playing at that level."

Beyond the chance to win, which included monetary prizes, Tina really appreciated the learning opportunities. "During the matches," she said, "there was also coaching during your time-outs. Everyone would come and chat with you about whom you're playing against and what you needed to do to win. After each event, you could ask the coaches for tips for improvement for the next matches based on what they saw. It gave you an incentive to get better."

Tina's Advice

I think I am a hard worker. I definitely study the game, I watch a lot of videos, and I listen to my coaches. But more than those strategies, you have to be ready to fail. You can't be afraid to suck. No person who wants to succeed does not fail first.

In pickleball, you can drive the ball as hard as you want, and you can get away with it up to a certain level. But then you have to learn a new skill and you're going to suck at it initially. People are going to beat you at rec play. You're going to feel really bad about yourself because you're not doing it perfectly. But with time and your own belief that it is the right thing to do, you will get better.

Fear is what stops people from developing their game. You have to get beyond the fear. You have to work at it even though it is just hard. So many people ask me how to improve their game. I tell them skill techniques are important, strategy is important, but the most important part is what is in your inner mind.

You can't do all of the tweaks and remember all of those plays if you keep saying you're not going to try because you're afraid you'll miss a shot. Unless you're playing in a tournament, I feel like you can try anything, because it doesn't really matter, except to your ego.

It is impossible to play perfect every day. I wish people would just give themselves a break. Some days you need to get off the court. Some days, your head is not in the game. There are other things in life that are happening for everybody outside of pickleball. You may just not be the person you thought you were going to be on the court that day. Move on, go to bed, wake up, do it again.

It's tough when you're not playing how you thought you would play. It's a bummer, but maybe people are outplaying you that day. You can pity yourself for a moment, but then that's gotta go. You will figure out what works and what doesn't, and you will become a better player.

While most of us won't become professional pickleball players, we all bring special talents to our game that gave us an edge over other players. Here are some thoughts from our everyday picklers.

Former tennis players already understand court placement and the mechanics of a racquet/paddle sport game, reducing their learning curve. When it comes to physical attributes, being tall and having a long reach can be an obvious advantage. Not as obvious is being left-handed, which can be helpful for court coverage with a right-handed player. It can be a secret weapon if the opponents don't notice and send a shot that normally would be to the player's backhand to the left-handed person's forehand.

Some pickleball skills our surveyed players think give them an edge are the third shot drop, proficiency with hitting very low shots, soft shots, excellent dinking ability, topspin shots, spin serves, and angle shots. Strategies for your best game include patience, self-confidence, the ability to play to your opponent's weakness, letting your opponent think you are a great player, intensity, competitiveness, and enthusiasm.

Chapter 8

Pickleball Lingo

Every sport has its terminology, and pickleball is no exception. There are some words unique to the sport that every beginning player needs to learn. Over time, pickleball players have invented expressions for special situations relating to the game.

How many of these terms do you know? Find one to work into the conversation at your next pickleball get together!

ATP (Around-the-Post Shot): You're dinking with your opponents and they pull you out wide. You hit a shot that goes around the post and not over the net. The ball lands in the court and your opponents can't hit it. This is known as an ATP shot. It would seem to be an illegal move—after all, the ball didn't even go over the net—but a shot around the post is indeed legal.

Body Shot or Body Bag: When the pickleball hits another player's body. This is legal and results in a point. Hitting your opponent with the ball accidentally (or on purpose) is one way to earn points and it is a strategy that is used in competitive pickleball.

Bounce It: Your partner will say this out loud if they want you to let the ball bounce, as it is likely to land out of bounds.

Cutthroat or Australian Doubles: This is a way to play pickleball with three players. The serving player plays against the other two players and only has to cover the serving half of the court. The server continues to serve and score points until two faults are made. Any hits by the receiving side to the non-serving area during that point are considered out of bounds. After two faults, the players rotate clockwise to assume new serving and receiving positions.

Dairy Queen (or DQ): A soft serve with a high loft, named after Dairy Queen's famous soft-serve ice cream. The term was popularized at Marie Courts in Mendota Heights, Minnesota.

Dink Shot or Drop Shot: This is a soft shot that lands in the kitchen or non-volley zone.

Divorce Alley: The area between two double partners is particularly appealing for opposing team members to direct shots at because each player may be expecting the other to hit the ball.

Erne Shot: An advanced pickleball shot where the player hits the ball either in the air as they jump around the kitchen lines or after establishing their feet just to the side of the kitchen. It is named after Erne Perry, who popularized the shot in competitive play.

Falafel: This is not your Middle Eastern food. A falafel in pickleball is a shot that doesn't reach its full potential, due to the player hitting the ball without any power.

Flapjack: A shot that must bounce once before it can be hit, such as when returning a serve.

Kitchen: Slang term for the non-volley zone. The area called the kitchen is the center of the court and the front of each side, closest to the net. It is seven feet from both sides of the net and from sideline to sideline. You may not volley from the kitchen area as that will earn you a fault. The term kitchen may have come from shuffleboard (you don't want to land your puck in the shuffleboard kitchen.) Everyone knows to stay out of the kitchen!

Lob: A high, arching shot hit to the opponent's backcourt. It may also be called a "lobster" or "lobster pot" or other annoying slang names indicating just how obnoxious this shot can be. The purpose of this shot is to make your opponents run for the ball and lose their positions.

Nasty Nelson: A seldom-used serve where the server tries to hit the opponent standing at the kitchen line and not the player receiving the serve. A serve that hits any opponent in the air wins a point for the serving team. This tactic, although appropriately named, is of questionable sportsmanship value. It was named after Tim Nelson.

Nice Setup: A nice setup means a player has successfully manipulated another to move to an area of the court, leaving an exposed section not covered by the opposing team, or when a player sets up his partner for an easy slam.

Nice Get: If someone on the court yells "nice get," this means that you hit a ball that was difficult to reach or return.

Nice Rally: This is a compliment to all players, meaning there has been a long streak of shots between teams. Pickleball players tend to complement their partner and their opponents.

No Man's Land: An area in the transition zone about two-third 2/3 of the way back from the net. This is usually used to describe a situation where players get caught between running up and hitting a longer shot, and often results in an error.

Out or Out of Bounds: Players may call a ball "out" when it is headed out of the court boundaries. This may either warn a partner not to hit it out of the air or tell the opponents it has been determined out of bounds. Players may also hold up one finger to signal the ball is out.

Paddle Tap: Tapping the butt of your paddle's handle to the other player's handle butt is a unique way to say "good game" to your opponents and partner at the end of a game.

Pickled: If a team scores zero points by the end of the game, they have been pickled. This is what you want to avoid.

Golden Pickle: The equivalent of a perfect game of pickleball. It occurs when the first team serving wins a game using its first serve only. The opposing team never scores a point and never even gets to serve!

Pickledome: The court where the championship match in a pickleball tournament is played.

Pickler: Someone who is obsessed with pickleball and cannot stop talking about the sport. A pickleball addict.

Poach: Poaching is where one team member will take the shot going toward their partner. Poaching typically results in a speed up or put away shot as a poach is an aggressive move that is meant to put pressure on your opponent.

Put Away: A ball that the opponent cannot return, therefore a winning shot.

Retirement: Even though pickleball may be your retirement game of choice, you won't want to call a retirement during a match. If you do so, it means you have decided to stop the match and award the point to your opponent.

Ricoshot: A shot that hits the net pole and ricochets into the opposing court. This is not a legal shot, but it is amusing.

Shadowing: A strategy used in doubles pickleball to work together as a team. Players move in sync to approach the net and to retreat. Imagine a rope is tied between partners—if one moves, the other must move.

Skinny Singles: A game played with two people, one on each side, using only half of the court usually cross-court from each other.

Slammers and Bangers: Slammers hit the ball hard and fast. A banger is a player that only hits hard drives and chooses power over placement.

Stacking: A strategy in doubles that teams can use to attempt the most advantageous court position based on each player's specific abilities. Stacking allows a team to maximize their strengths.

Third Shot Drop: The elusive pickleball shot that all pickle-ballers must learn to achieve to take their game to the next level. It is the shot taken after a return of the serve that is strategically placed in the opponent's kitchen.

Tweener: The term used when the ball from the opposing team is shot between your legs. It has also been called "being pickled" in certain regional areas.

Volley Llama: Players illegally attack balls when their feet are in the non-volley zone during gameplay.

YIPS: An unexplainable sudden inability to perform routine skills by an experienced athlete in their sport. It is an acronym which came from the golfing world, but it has become a universal term that can happen in any sport. It stands for "You idiot, putt straight!"

John's Story

In my case, the YIPS centered around my serving skills in pickleball. It happened when I was playing with some beginning players. I felt that a fast serve wouldn't be fun for anyone. So, I changed the speed and motion of my serve to soften the game so that everyone could enjoy a good return. This made the game fun and competitive.

When I returned to playing at full speed a few weeks later, it was nearly impossible for me to get a serve in the box. Before I got the serving YIPS, I was able to execute 100% of my serves and I was able to place them strategically in the box. I had to begin the process of trying to get my serve back. As a former tournament golf player, I know it is not uncommon for a player to experience the putting YIPS. It can happen at any time and especially as you get older. In both sports, it seems to be more mental than physical.

First, I tried different grips, stances, eye locations, weight distribution, and anything else that came to mind. It seemed that when it was time for the moment of contact, my brain questioned my ability to complete a successful serve. This resulted in failure to execute the serve.

I went straight to YouTube and watched as many videos about serving techniques in pickleball as I could. I would watch a video and then head to the courts to hit hundreds of serves while no one was watching. I even videotaped my sessions. In the rain, the cold, early morning, and late at night, I would practice.

When asked to play, I was afraid to let my partner down, so I would usually decline. If I agreed to play, I would become anxious the night before thinking about my serve. Even after all the successful practice sessions by myself, I still could not get a serve anywhere near in the receiving square.

The YIPS speeds everything up, and your motion becomes out of sequence. You are so worried about the outcome that you forget about the process. People feel your pain, and they try to help by giving you great tips, but they don't work. A lot of effort is required to retrain your brain.

I decided to try a few new techniques. The pre-shot routine was the most important, which included slowing my brain down, bouncing the ball a few times, and picturing everything in slow motion. I would drop the ball and try to hit it when it was standing still like in tennis. Then I would hit the ball and follow through. One video suggested when you hit the ball, pretend there are three balls to hit and it will cause you to follow through.

Eventually I got my serves in and began to build my confidence back. I just had to believe I could do it!

Side Out

LOB

KITCHEN

Poach

Around the Post

YIPS

Drop Shot

ERNE

Dink

Chapter 9

Pickleball Party Time

Let's celebrate with a pickleball party!

What is a pickleball party, you ask? A pickleball party can be focused on playing pickleball and creating a party around the play, or it can be a pickleball-themed event with food and decorations all geared toward the sport.

Pickleball parties can celebrate big life events, such as a birthday or retirement, but you can also host one for just about any reason you want! Won a game? Increased your DUPR score? Got a new pickleball outfit? All of these are excellent reasons to have a pickleball party! It would also be the perfect way to celebrate National Pickleball Day on August 8.

Just like the sport, pickleball parties are a great way to have people come together socially. A pickleball playing party could be held at a court facility, a public park with pickleball courts, a private club with courts, a party room, or even your own driveway with a portable net and marked off court lines.

Here are some helpful ideas for your next pickleball party. Let's get this party planning started!

Pickleball Decorations

Party decorations are a huge part of your pickleball party's atmosphere and theme. It may be challenging to find pickleball-specific decorations at your local party store, but more choices are popping up all the time, especially online. You may need to get creative.

Most pickleball-themed DIY decorations are pretty straightforward and don't require expert crafting skills. The main goal should be to highlight the typical images associated with pickleball. Paddles, the pickleball court, and pickleballs are your primary sources of inspiration.

It is easy to incorporate real pickleballs and paddles into your decorations:

- *Place pickleballs at the end of long skewers and nestle them in among your flower arrangements.*
- *Fill a clear flower vase with regular or mini pickleballs before adding the flowers.*
- *Make a pickleball wreath by binding together several pickleballs in the shape of a wreath. Attach other items, such as a pickleball paddle, with glue or wire.*
- *Put mini pickleballs in a sherbet glass and set them on the food table.*
- *Purchase a strand of mini pickleballs that light up to add a festive touch to your décor.*

Pickleball-Themed Food

You can't have a party without food! Get creative with pickle-themed foods, such as sliders with a pickle relish special sauce or Cuban sandwiches with lots of pickles on them. Dill pickle dip, fried pickles, pickles in a blanket, and pickle-packed potato salad are a few yummy suggestions. A variety of recipes perfect for any pickleball part can be found at the end of this chapter.

Besides the obvious connection to the sport, pickles really are the perfect party and post-match bite. They're refreshing and the brine is full of restorative electrolytes.

Charcuterie boards are incredibly popular at parties these days and it would be easy to include a variety of pickles. You could even take it to the next level and use a pickleball paddle as the base for your charcuterie board.

This board was made with a sweet and a savory side. The savory side has Swiss cheese and mini pickles. The sweet side has chocolate mini-paddles and pickleball Oreo truffles. Even the net is edible. It is made of chocolate and pretzels, the perfect salty and sweet snack.

Credit: Kirsten Nunez for ehow

There are many clever ways to incorporate pickleball into a cake design:

- Create pickleball cupcakes by decorating the round tops to resemble a bright yellow pickleball!.

- Make bite-sized cake pops decorated as pickleballs.

- Decorate a sheet cake to resemble a pickleball court using icing, plastic cake decorating elements, or candy melts to create a net.

Pickleball-Themed Drinks

If your party includes a crowd of adults, you must have a pickleball cocktail (or a mocktail, if you prefer). Craft a Dirty Martini that fits the theme by using pickle juice instead of olive juice and garnishing with a gherkin. Serve a classic Bloody Mary with a pickle spear. Daniel Rivkin, a mixologist and pickleball player, has created several themed cocktails with clever names like The Kitchen Sink, Dirty Pickle-tini, and Punch Shot Punch, and a mocktail called The Pink Dink. All of these recipes are at the end of this chapter.

Pickleball Party Favors

Party favors give your guests something to remember all the fun they had at your party. Personalized t-shirts, cups, and unique paddle covers are more expensive treats. Bottle openers, pickleball towels, pickleball bag tags, magnets, stickers, mini pickleball wine stoppers can all be found online.

Aside from party favors, consider giving out trophies to guests who either win party games or participate in the party's pickleball tournament. A jar of pickles with a pickleball glued on the lid can make a fun and funny trophy gift. If you're planning on hosting a pickleball tournament as part of the party, your guests will be excited to compete for something special to take home!

Pickleball Activities

Every party needs a few games and activities to entertain your guests! For a pickleball-themed party, mini games can add to the party fun.

Here are a few suggestions:

- *Pickleball juggling*
- *A contest of who can balance a pickleball on their head for the longest time*
- *A relay race with a pickleball on a spoon*
- *Cornhole with pickleball beanbags*
- *Pickleball trivia—a great way to practice teamwork to see which team reigns as the most knowledgeable pickleball group. Try to make your questions range in difficulty so that everyone feels like they have a chance to contribute. Questions can be simple like, "What is a dink?" and "What is another term for the non-volley zone?" or more challenging like, "What is a Nasty Nelson?"*

Pickleball Party Tournament Ideas

If your party is centered around playing pickleball, your party tournament doesn't need to be as big or as serious as a major tournament, but it does need to be an organized event. A little friendly competition will keep your guests interested in the games and add a great sense of excitement to your party's atmosphere.

A perfect way to make sure everyone gets to know each other better is by doing a mixer-style tournament. In a mixer, each game is played in the doubles format, and players rotate to a different team every game. This way each guest gets the chance to meet new people. Another fun tournament idea is to do a round-robin tournament where teams are determined by matching pickleball beginners with more experienced players.

In this format, new players can compete while learning the nuances of the game from their more experienced partners. Each team will compete against one another to see who will win the grand prize. Of course, the grand prize will be something special like water bottles saying, "Tears of my opponents!"

Just like the sport of pickleball, the main goal of a pickleball party is to have fun!

Air Fryer Fried Pickles

Ingredients:

2 cups dill pickle slices
½ cup flour
1 large egg
1 tablespoon water
½ cup breadcrumbs
¼ cup grated Parmesan
1 tablespoon Italian seasoning

Instructions:

1. Place the pickles on a paper towel and pat dry.
2. Using three small bowls, add the flour to the first bowl. In the second bowl, add the egg and whisk it with the water. In the last bowl, add the breadcrumbs, Parmesan, and Italian seasoning.
3. Dip each pickle in the flour, then dredge in the egg mixture and then in the bread crumb mixture.
4. Lay the pickles in a single layer in the air fryer basket.
5. Cook at 400°F for 8–10 minutes.
6. Goes great with ranch dressing or your favorite dipping sauce.

Makes 4 servings

Special Sauce For Pickleball Sliders

Ingredients:

1/2 cup mayonnaise

2 tablespoons ketchup

2 teaspoons sweet pickle relish or 4 chopped bread & butter
  pickles

1 teaspoon spicy brown mustard

1 teaspoon Worcestershire sauce

Ground black pepper to taste

Instructions:

1. Mix first five: ingredients together, taste, then add
    pepper as needed.
2. Grill, bake, or air fry your favorite mini meat patty or
    protein substitute.
3. Put a dollop on the top and bottom of the slider bun and
    add the protein.

Dill Pickle Dip

Ingredients:

4 ounces cream cheese, softened
½ cup sour cream
¾ cup pickles, diced
2 tablespoons pickle juice
2 tablespoons green onions, sliced
1 tablespoon dill fresh, chopped with stems removed
¼ teaspoon garlic powder
¼ teaspoon kosher salt

Instructions:

1. Using a mixer, beat the cream cheese until it is very smooth.
2. Blend the rest of the ingredients using the mixer except for the salt. Then add salt if needed.
3. Serve with your favorite fresh vegetables, crackers, or chips.
4. Can be made one day ahead

Makes about 1 ½ cups of dip, enough for 8 servings

Pickles In A Pocket

Ingredients:

24 slices of salami
24 mini gherkins
Herb cream cheese, such as Alouette or Boursin

Instructions:

1. Paint each salami slice with the herb cream cheese.
2. Place pickle on top of the cream cheese in the middle.
3. Fold up each side of the salami, overlap, and secure with a toothpick.

Makes 24

PICKLEball Potato Salad

Ingredients:

2 pounds red potatoes, cut into bite sized pieces
2 hard-boiled eggs, chopped
1 cup mayonnaise
½ cup sour cream
1 tablespoon spicy brown mustard
1 teaspoon kosher salt
½ teaspoon ground black pepper
2 stalks chopped celery or 1/2 teaspoon celery salt
¼ cup dill pickles with juices, chopped
¼ cup sweet pickles with juices, chopped or pickle relish
2 green onions, chopped
2 tablespoons dill pickle brine

Instructions:

1. In a large stockpot, cover potatoes with water and bring potatoes to a boil over medium-high heat. Reduce heat, and simmer until fork tender, about 15-20 minutes. Drain and let cool slightly.
2. In a large bowl, stir together mayonnaise, sour cream, mustard, salt, and pepper. Pour over potatoes and gently stir until combined.
3. Add celery or celery salt, dill pickles, sweet pickles or relish, green onions, and brine. Gently stir until combined.
4. Cover and refrigerate for at least four hours before serving.

Makes 8 servings

Down The Middle MeatBALLS

Ingredients:

32 ounces frozen fully cooked meatballs
1 cup grape jelly
1 ½ cup barbecue sauce
2 tablespoons chili sauce

Instructions:

1. Add the frozen meatballs, grape jelly, barbecue sauce, and chili sauce into the slow cooker. Mix until well combined.
2. Cover and cook on low for 3-4 hours, stirring halfway through cooking. Keep covered and on the warm setting until ready to serve.

Makes 12 appetizer servings

Cocktails [4]

Traditional Shandy

Ingredients:

1:1 lager to lemonade
Lemon slice, for garnish

Instructions:

1. Pour beer into a tall glass.
2. Add lemonade.
3. Garnish with lemon wedge.

The Kitchen Sink

Ingredients:

4 sprigs fresh mint
2 ounces simple syrup
2 ounces gin
2 ounces vodka
2 ounces light rum
2 ounces triple sec
8 ounces soda water, plain or citrus
4 lime wedges, for garnish

Instructions:

1. Muddle the mint in the cocktail shaker.
2. Add the spirits and shake vigorously.
3. Strain into iced glasses.
4. Finish with soda and a lime garnish.

Dirty Pickletini

Ingredients:

3 ounces gin or vodka
2 ounces dry vermouth
1 ounce pickle juice
1 ounce framboise liqueur for depth.
1 quartered pickle, for garnish

Instructions:

1. Add all ingredients to a cocktail shaker with ice and shake.
2. Pour into martini glasses and garnish with a pickle of your choice.

Punch Shot Punch

Ingredients:

2 ounces dark pineapple rum
1 ounce spiced rum or light rum
1 ounce Falernum
1 ounce peach liqueur, not schnapps
½ ounce lime juice
½ ounce lemon juice
2 dashes Peychaud's bitters
1 dash aromatic bitters
1 pineapple wedge, for garnish

Instructions:

1. Mix all ingredients in a shaker
2. Pour over crushed ice
3. Garnish with pineapple wedge

The Pink Dink Mocktail

Ingredients:

2 ½ ounces peach juice
2 ½ ounces strawberry lemonade
2 ½ ounces lemon soda water or Sprite or 7UP
1 splash grenadine syrup

Instructions:

1. Combine the peach juice and strawberry lemonade in an iced shaker.
2. Pour into a tall glass filled with ice and add the lemon flavored soda water.
3. Add the grenadine.

Appendix

1972: A corporation was formed to protect the creation of this new sport.

1976: The first pickleball tournament was held at the South Center Athletic Club in Tukwila, Washington. The men's doubles winners were Scott Stover and Rob Cahill.

1984: The United States Amateur Pickleball Association was organized. Their goal was to continue the growth and advancement of pickleball on a national level. The first rulebook was published in March 1984. The first composite paddle was made by Arlen Paranto, a Boeing Industrial Engineer.

1990: Pickleball was being played in all 50 states.

1999: The first pickleball internet website, Pickleball Stuff, was launched to give fans a central place for information and equipment.

2005: USA Pickleball Association was established and a US-APA website was created. USAPA became a nonprofit and was instrumental in creating a single reliable database for players to find sites to play. Today, the website is places2play. org. Earl Hill, a charter member of the USAPA Board, founded the Ambassador Program in 2005. Ambassadors are volunteer representatives and unofficial spokespersons for the USAPA whose primary responsibility is to promote and grow pickleball in the geographical area they represent.

2008: The USAPA Rules Committee published the USA Pickleball Association Official Tournament Rulebook (revision, May 1, 2008). Pickleball was included for the first time at the National Senior Games Association.

2009: The first USAPA National Tournament for players of all ages was held in Buckeye, Arizona.

2010: The USAPA established the International Federation of Pickleball (IFP) organization to encourage the growth of the sport on an international level.

2014: The Pickleball Channel was launched. It was the first professional media group for the sport.

2016: USAPA created a national certified referee program. Pickleball Magazine was launched as the first print and digital publication for the sport.

2017: USAPA and the International Pickleball Teaching Professional Association (IPTPA) started a Pickleball Hall of Fame. The USAPA National Championships had a two-hour segment broadcasted on the CBS Sports Network.

2018: USAPA partnered with pickleballtournaments.com to produce the sport's first results-based tournament player ratings (UTPRs). The Professional Pickleball Registry (PPR) was formed as a subsidiary of the Professional Tennis Registry (PTR). This registry certified over 1000 new pickleball instructors in the first six months. The Margaritaville USA Pickleball National Championships were broadcast on ESPNEWS. The cash prize was $75,000 for the event.

2019: The National Championships put an emphasis on the spectator experience and established a VIP lounge with live video screens just outside the stadium court. Nearly 28,000 fans attended.

2020: USAPA was rebranded as USA Pickleball with a new logo and an updated website. The goal was to project the image as the official pickleball organization in the U.S.

2021: USA pickleball membership ended the year with 53,000 members, up 43% from 2020.

2021: National Pickleball Day was created by Deirdre Morris, a pickleball instructor.

Notes

1. Gay, Jason, "John McEnroe Is Playing Pickleball for
   $1 Million? You Cannot Be Serious," *The Wall Street
   Journal*, March 30, 2023, https://www.wsj.com.

2. Peterson, Mark et al, "Grip Strength Is Inversely
   Associated with DNA Methylation Age Acceleration,"
   Journal of Cachexia, Sarcopenia, and Muscle,
   November 9, 2022.

3. Layton, Jeff and DeBeliso, Mark, "Is There a Relationship
   between Maximal Grip Strength and Racquetball
   Success? A Pilot Study," *Athens Journal of Sports*,
   Vol. 4, No. 2, June 2017.

4. Rivkin, Daniel, "Bottoms Up: 6 Pickleball-Inspired
   Beverages to Up Your Bar Game", *IntoPickleball*,
   https://intopickleball.com/bottoms-up/.

5. "The History of the Game," https://usapickleball.org.

Share your pickleball story with us at
www.theheartofpickleball.com